THE POWER IN REASON

quick **PRO**
guides

THE POWER IN REASON

Andrew Eisele

Hal Leonard Books

An Imprint of Hal Leonard Corporation

Published in 2012 by Hal Leonard Books
An Imprint of Hal Leonard Corporation
7777 West Bluemound Road
Milwaukee, WI 53213

Trade Book Division Editorial Offices
33 Plymouth St., Montclair, NJ 07042

Book design by Adam Fulrath
Book composition by Bill Gibson

Library of Congress Cataloging-in-Publication Data

Eisele, Andrew.
  The power in Reason / by Andrew Eisele.
     p. cm. – (QuickPro series)
  Includes bibliographical references.
 1. Reason (Computer file) 2. Software synthesizers. 3. Software samplers. 4. Software sequencers. I. Title.
  ML74.4.R43E37 2011
  781.3'4536–dc23
                          2011029767

Printed in the United States of America

ISBN 978-1-45840-228-8

www.halleonardbooks.com

CONTENTS

Chapter 3

Chapter 4

Chapter 5

Chapter 6

Chapter 7

Chapter 8

Chapter 9

Chapter 10

Chapter 11

Chapter 12

Contents

Chapter 1

SETTING UP YOUR STUDIO FOR REASON

Before diving into the tutorials that will instruct you on the basics, let's first have a look at the system requirements for running Reason. I've also compiled some information with regard to the kind of equipment you may wish to consider purchasing to get the most out of your computer-based studio. These recommendations are based on my own personal experience, so by all means, do your own research and, if possible, check out the product before purchasing. Most major music retailers will have this type of gear available and often have showrooms in which you can test out products. Also make sure the store from which you are purchasing has a decent return policy in the event you are unsatisfied with your decision.

Prerequisites for Running Reason

To effectively run Reason you will need a computer that meets the following minimum requirements.

Computer

Mac OS X

- Intel Mac (multiple cores highly recommended)
- 1 GB RAM or more
- DVD drive
- Mac OS X 10.4 or later
- 2 GB free hard disk space
- Monitor with 1024x768 resolution or larger
- Core Audio compliant audio interface or built-in audio hardware
- A MIDI interface and a MIDI keyboard recommended

Windows

- Intel Pentium 4/AMD Athlon or better
- 1GB RAM
- DVD drive
- Windows XP SP3, Vista, or Windows 7
- 2 GB free hard disk space
- Monitor with 1024x768 resolution or larger
- A 16-bit Windows-compatible audio card, preferably with an ASIO driver
- A MIDI interface and a MIDI keyboard recommended</UL>

Audio Interface

It is possible to run Reason with the built-in sound card that comes with your computer; however, it is recommended that you invest in a proper audio interface, as this will allow your computer to perform better when recording and playing back audio. It will also alleviate much of the headaches associated with working with subpar equipment. You are looking for an audio interface that meets the demands of digital audio. Audio interfaces that are designed for gaming are not always adequate. Luckily, there are a number of low-cost options on the market, so with a little effort you should be able to easily find something suitable.

FireWire

FireWire is a technology that allows for fast data throughput and greater performance. My favorite low-cost interface is the Apogee Duet. It features two microphone inputs, two line inputs, two line outputs, and MIDI I/O (input and output). It also features two high-quality microphone preamps. This unit usually sells for just under $500 brand new. It's the best bang for the buck as there's really nothing else of this quality in this price rage. Apogee has just released the Duet 2, so you could also look for sales on the original.

Other manufacturers of FireWire interfaces are MOTU, M-Audio, PreSonus, RME Hammerfall, Focusrite, and TC Electronics.

USB

USB stands for "universal serial bus" and is the most popular connection for computers today. There are a number of USB audio interfaces on the market, but I highly recommend using an interface with USB 2 or higher as the data through put is much faster (on par with or faster than FireWire). Specifically I recommend the Apogee Duet 2, as the sound quality is still superior to anything in its price range.

Other manufacturers of USB interfaces are MOTU, M-Audio, PreSonus, RME Hammerfall, Focusrite, TC Electronics, Native Instruments, Avid/Digidesign, Mackie, and Alesis.

MIDI Interface

A MIDI interface is usually a USB device with one or more inputs and outputs, which allows for the connection of MIDI equipment such as keyboards and synthesizers. Fortunately, most audio interfaces have built-in MIDI interfaces. There are also MIDI controllers that have built-in MIDI interfaces and connect directly to your computer via USB.

MOTU, Cakewalk, Roland, Midisport, and M-Audio are popular manufacturers of MIDI interfaces.

Monitors (Speakers)

A studio monitor is designed to give you an accurate representation of your music and is often calibrated to have a "flat" frequency response. It is possible to use regular hi-fi audio speakers or bookshelf speakers from your home stereo, but more often than not, the consumer speakers are designed to make the music sound "better" with the use of digital processing. This is fine if you are just listening to music. For example, commercially released CDs should sound great on these systems. However, if you are actively mixing a song, this playback system is not ideal as, due to the calibration, it will fool you and your mixing won't translate to other playback systems. Your music might sound fine on your home stereo, but listening to it in your car or via a club system, you'll discover that your mixes often won't sound the same.

There are two types of studio monitors, passive and active.

Passive

Passive monitors are usually a little cheaper, but they require the use of an audio amplifier, which is an additional expense and will take up extra room in your studio.

Active

Active monitors have the amplifier built into the speaker. This is a space saver and has the additional benefit of the manufacturer's building the amplifiers to match the speakers perfectly, resulting in better performance and sound quality.

Subwoofer

Depending on the type of music you are producing and the size of your studio monitors, you may wish to invest in a subwoofer, which is a low-frequency speaker capable of producing powerful bass. Designed to pick up where your studio monitors leave off, subwoofers will help immensely when producing bass-heavy music such as hip-hop, drum and bass, dubstep, cumbia, glitch, electro house, techno, and other forms of electronic music.

There are a number of manufacturers of studio monitors. Some even package subwoofers as part of a set. Check out KRK, Event, Genelec, Tannoy, M-Audio, Blue Sky, Yamaha, and Dynaudio.

Headphones

Headphones are a good investment, as they will allow you to work without bothering loved ones and neighbors. They can also give you a different take on your mix. However, they are not an adequate replacement for a good pair of studio monitors. Look for good quality, comfort, and ones that don't overemphasize bass frequencies. My personal favorites are the Sony MDR 7506. They usually cost about $99 and sound great without overhyping the bass. Also, FocusRite just released the VRM Box, which uses DSP (digital signal processing) to emulate different studio monitors from within your headphones. The wonders of modern technology!

Other manufacturers of headphones include Sennheiser, AKG, Audio-Technica, Sure, and Beyerdynamic.

Controllers

MIDI controllers come in all sorts of shapes and sizes, from MIDI guitars, keyboards, and drum pads to full-size harps and pianos. If you own a keyboard or synthesizer that has a MIDI output, you can use this in conjunction with a MIDI interface. Most audio interfaces also have a MIDI input, which would be a replacement for a dedicated MIDI interface. A simpler solution is to use a USB controller.

Keyboard

USB MIDI keyboard controllers aren't an absolute must if you wish to produce music in Reason, but I highly recommend using one, as it speeds up the process of recording MIDI. Keyboard controllers come in various sizes, some with more features than others.

I recommend finding a controller that has at least a two-octave range with velocity sensitivity and dedicated pitch bend and modulation control.

Some manufacturers include M-Audio, Novation, Akai, Yamaha, Korg, Roland, and Alesis.

Control Surface (Mixing)

Another USB controller used to control mix parameters is the control surface. It is a dedicated controller that often looks like a mixing board, but no audio passes through it, as it's used to control software parameters. These range in price from $50 (Korg nanoKONTROL) to over $20K (SSL Matrix). It's nice to have the hands-on control for mixing, but I find that it's not a necessity. Check out Novation Zero SL for a good-quality control surface.

Microphone

If you are planning on recording your own samples in Reason, you'll need a good-quality microphone. Fortunately, a number of low-cost microphones are available on the market. Several types are available, the most popular being the dynamic and condenser.

Dynamic

A dynamic microphone is a great, all-purpose microphone. These are often used in both live sound and studio recording. They are hardy and very rarely break unless seriously abused. Shure, Audix, AKG, Audio-Technica, and Sennhieser make great dynamic microphones.

Condenser

Condenser microphones are most often used in recording studios. They are extremely sensitive and perfect for home recording; however, they do require a microphone preamplifier with power (48 volts—often referred to as phantom power). Fortunately, most audio interfaces have microphone preamps with phantom power built into them. Because of their sensitivity, they need to be handled with care. They can break if dropped, but if properly cared for, can last a lifetime. Røde, Studio Projects, Cascade, MXL, Blue, Audio-Technica, and Sure are just a few manufacturers of inexpensive, high-quality condenser microphones.

Microphone Accessories

Microphone Stand

Be sure to invest in a mic stand. Budget ones are fine, but can break over time. I prefer a tripod stand with a boom extension, as this allows for greater flexibility when recording.

Microphone Cable

Cables come in a variety of lengths and quality. I've been making my own cables for years, but if you're not handy with a soldering iron, invest in the lowest tier of a quality manufacturer such as Monster or Mogami.

Pop Filter

If you were planning on recording vocals, it would be wise to invest in a pop filter. This will help prevent "plosives" (excessive p's and t's) from ruining a recording. There are some name brands, but I've always been happy with the inexpensive no-name brand usually costing about $20.

Other Accessories

Power Conditioner

Although not a necessity, a power conditioner with surge protection is a great investment. These typically are either the channel strip type or studio rack mounts and will offer multiple A/C plugs (usually eight plugs). Depending on the specs, they can condition the power to cut down on electronic noise created by appliances in your home or studio. Some offer protection from power spikes and lightning (however, I still unplug my gear during electrical storms). Some manufacturers offer insurance, so if something does go wrong, they can help with replacing the damaged equipment. Some power conditioners even have battery backup, so if you lose power, you've got a few minutes to save and turn off your computer properly.

Furman, ETA, Monster, and APC are a few manufacturers of power conditioners.

Cables

One often overlooked aspect of your studio is cables. When purchasing your software and hardware, make sure that you don't forget to buy the right cables. There are a number of manufacturers of cables. As I said in the microphone section, I prefer to make my own, but if you're not handy with a soldering iron, invest in the lowest tier of a quality manufacturer such as Monster or Mogami.

That said, keep your cable runs as short as possible. Don't buy a twenty-five-foot cable if you only need ten feet. Longer cables may add interference. Also, when in doubt, use balanced cables (XLR or TRS). This will help cut down on noise and interference, especially when working over long distances.

Setting Up Your Studio

Selecting Your Room

When selecting a space to install your studio, look for a room without parallel walls or ceiling if possible. Odd-shaped rooms with slanted ceilings (such as an attic) are great for a mixing environment. The last thing you want is a perfectly square room where the walls, ceiling, and floor are equidistant. If this is not possible, buying some room treatment to help with reflections will help your mixing environment.

Room Treatment

There are a number of manufacturers of room treatment materials available for purchase. Prime Acoustics, Real Traps, Auralex, and Clearsonic are a few manufacturers.

Another low-cost alternative is using compressed fiberglass (the same material used in air ducts). This can be purchased from a home store such as Home Depot. I recommend framing with wood, covering with material, and hanging on your walls and on the ceiling above the mix position.

Room Correction

Another option for getting the best mixing environment is the advent of room correction hardware/software. These typically come with a special calibration microphone that works with software to analyze your room's acoustics and correct any issues found. This is not a necessity for you to use Reason, but will help your mixes sound their best.

IK Multimedia, KRK, and JBL offer room correction packages.

Setting Up Your Mix Position

Once you've got your equipment, I recommend setting your studio monitors equidistant from your head in the mix position. The ideal position is to have the high-frequency drivers (tweeters) at ear level and measured in equal distances between your left and right monitors. You're trying to create an equilateral triangle between your monitor and your ears. For instance, if your monitors are spaced four feet apart, then the optimum mix position is four feet from the monitors. Use of a tape measure is recommended, as the precision of the distance is required.

Hooking Up Your Monitors

Connect your audio cables to your audio interface. The Left output (Output 1) connects to the Left monitor as it faces you. The Right output (Output 2) connects to the Right monitor as it faces you.

Installing Drivers

If your audio interface is class compliant, your computer should recognize it automatically. But, if your interface requires drivers, I recommend going to the manufacturer's Web site and checking the latest version of the drivers. If the Web site has newer software available, skip the CD that ships with the product and install the newer software from the Web site.

The same process applies your MIDI interface or MIDI controller. Always check the manufacturer's Web site before installing from a CD.

Check to see if your device is available on your computer.

On a PC, this will usually be displayed at the bottom right corner of the screen, or you can check the Control Panel for the devices.

On the Mac, open the AMS (audio MIDI setup) found in the Utilities folder within the Applications folder. Once open, your devices should be present in their respective windows (Audio Devices and MIDI Studio).

Installing Reason

Reason uses copy protection that is based on disk verification and license number authorization.

Be sure to keep your disks and license number safe. Also prompt registration of your product is recommended. It allows you access to the latest version of the software, and if your disks are lost or damaged, you'll be eligible for replacement disks. If you do not register Reason and your disks are stolen or lost, then you are facing having to repurchase the software.

Setting Up Preferences

Before you can begin to use Reason, you must first set up your preferences, which will allow Reason to communicate with your peripherals.

The setup wizard asks you questions about your audio interface and MIDI keyboard controller and will set things up for you.

If by chance you didn't have your hardware set up or you'd like to make some changes to your setup, you'll want to be familiar with the Preferences selection process. On rare occasions, Reason may lose communication with your MIDI controller and/or audio interface and you will need to reselect the options in Preferences.

As a result, it's a good idea to become familiar with the process of selecting your preferences.

Let's begin by launching Reason. Once open, select Preferences from the Reason drop-down menu.

General Preferences

Under this first tab, you can set a lot of Reason's behavior and the visual look of the program. It also gives you options on how the program should open. This page can be left in its default state. However, please direct your attention to the Default Song section. You'll keep the default—Built In—for now, but will be changing this after your Reason Overview.

Built In

This option opens Reason with a mixer, ready to build a song from scratch.

Empty Rack

Opens Reason with a "blank" rack.

Custom

This setting allows for setting up a song start or template file, which is useful for a quick song start. When you first launch Reason, this is the default setting, with Demo Song selected.

Open Last Song on Startup

This opens the last project you were working on in the previous session.

Next, select the drop-down menu at the top of the page, which currently says General. Select the next option, Audio.

Audio Preferences

By default, the audio device is set to No Sound.

Press the drop-down menu and select your audio device.

If you don't see your audio interface listed, make sure you've downloaded the current drivers or contact the manufacturer.

In this figure I have selected Built-in Input + Built-in Output for my audio device.

Other Audio Options to Consider

Sample Rate—Reason supports sample rates from 44,100 up to 96,000. You're going to use the default 44,100 sample rate.

Buffer Size—This slider increases or decreases your buffer size. Let's leave this at the default setting of 512 samples.

Latency and Buffer Size

Latency is a delay that is caused by the processing of data. In regard to your audio system, it takes a certain amount of time for a computer to capture, process, and send audio information. The time this process takes is directly related to the buffer size. A higher buffer setting may result in an audible delay. This can manifest in a delay when pressing a note on your MIDI controller, which makes playing and recording difficult. A delay may also manifest when recording audio.

Imagine setting up a microphone and strumming a guitar, only you hear the guitar one second after you've played it. By setting a lower buffer setting, you're able to reduce the delay to an acceptable amount and allow yourself to play along in real time.

As you build your song, you'll inevitably use several tracks with effects, and with the addition of virtual instruments, it won't be long before your computer's processor is overtaxed. The result is slow, sluggish response with crackles, pops, and audio dropouts. To compensate for this you must increase the buffer, thereby increasing latency. Most audio interfaces today produce very good results. The idea is to find a good balance with buffer settings to allow acceptable performance with lower latencies. I tend to use a lower buffer setting when recording and then increase the buffer setting when mixing.

Let's move back to the Preference drop-down menu and select Keyboards and Control Surfaces.

Keyboards and Control Surfaces

Select Auto-detect Surfaces.

Reason will first scan your computer for any available MIDI interfaces and keyboard controllers. If your controller does not show up under Auto-detect, select the Add button, and manually choose the manufacturer and model of your controller.

If you multiple controllers are found and you only wish to use one in particular, then deselect Use with Reason for any controller you don't wish to use with Reason.

Keep the Standard option for the master keyboard input. Using multiple controllers will be explored in the live performance chapter of the QuickPro Reason Advanced book.

Advanced MIDI

This preference is used to set up Reason for use with external sequencers. It offers four banks of sixteen channels, giving you a total of sixty-four MIDI channels work with. This function is beyond the scope of this series.

Computer Keyboard

Reason features a piano keyboard that is controlled by the QWERTY keyboard (computer's keyboard). This utility gives us a virtual MIDI keyboard controller. It's a fantastic way to record MIDI or audition sounds when a proper MIDI keyboard controller is not available. The preferences allow for the customization of the setup of the QWERTY keyboard. For your purposes, the default setting is fine. The computer keyboard can be accessed by selecting F4 on your QWERTY keyboard or by selecting Show On-screen Piano Keys from the Windows drop-down window on the Reason menu.

Chapter 2
REASON OVERVIEW

Finding the right software application for proper musical production can be quite a challenge, especially when you need one that is as powerful as it is easy to use yet operates smoothly on even the most basic computer setups, and includes all the virtual tools required for making music in just about every possible style. Congratulations for making Reason your software of choice. Without question, Reason is one of the most powerful yet easy-to-use music-making software applications available today. For example, consider how just the massive collection of instruments and effects available in Reason alone has revolutionized individual music production. Prior to its introduction in 2000, obtaining all of these instruments and effects required the purchase of separate hardware, literally costing several thousand dollars, in addition to costly hardware sequencers or expensive sequencing software to even utilize these tools. However, the introduction of Reason by Propellerhead changed all this by enabling individual production of electronic music easily and effectively with simply a personal computer, a simple MIDI controller, and adequate monitoring. The tools and instruments included in Reason enable anyone to achieve professional music production results easily and effectively without such additional costs or hardware. Now in its fifth incarnation, this powerful studio tool, upgraded with a vast array of samplers, drum machines, synths, and so much more, gives you all the tools you need to produce professional-quality music.

Furthermore, with this QuickPro guide, which has been specifically designed to get you up and running quickly and efficiently, you will be producing music easily in no time, without having to overlearn every detail or spend inordinate time learning the basics. In short, this book is not a mere rehash of the instruction manual; rather, it is a focused guide created to rapidly bring you up to speed on the basics so you can transition seamlessly into mastering the advanced production techniques, enabling you can take full advantage of all the benefits this amazing music production software has to offer.

But before you begin your journey into the ins and outs of Reason, let's start with an overview of the concept of MIDI!

What Is MIDI?

MIDI (musical instrument digital interface) is a universal programming protocol that was adopted as the music industry standard by every major manufacturer of electronic instruments since the early '80s to standardize parameters dealing with musical production. Prior to MIDI, every manufacturer had already developed its own unique means of communication regarding its respective products; however this, in turn, created much difficulty on the user end by requiring multiple methods for varying instruments or devices to be used simultaneously. The MIDI protocol created standardized settings for information, such as note volume, pitch, velocity, aftertouch, and so on, thereby enabling compatibility across all products.

One of the most important concepts to consider with regard to MIDI is that it contains no audio data. When you record MIDI data, the variables performance, not the actual audio waveforms, are the primary focus. Once recorded, the MIDI data parameters can then be edited into the desired performance effect with a variety of enhancement tools. For example, if you wish to edit a particular variable such as the pitch or key of the instrument, you have just recorded, with audio waveforms you would need to rerecord the entire instrumentation sample to change or enhance certain variables. However, with MIDI, you simply adjust just the patch of the instrument or even change the instrument itself, without having to rerecord. This then makes editing an incredibly easy, flexible, and even fun process, thereby making even the most minute adjustment to any variable a breeze.

What Is Reason?

Reason, in a nutshell, is the software version of a MIDI production suite, or a virtual studio. Replete with a plethora of synthesizers, drum machines, samplers, and effects, this software is broken up into two easy-to-understand main windows. The first is called the rack and the second is the sequencer. The former is designed to visually look like a nineteen-foot rack mount case that houses all of the instruments and effects required to produce quality music. The sequencer, by default, is positioned underneath the bottom of the rack and is used to record and play back all the MIDI data.

Let's begin your tour of the software by opening up the demo song. When you first launch the software, the default song, aptly named Demo Song, will automatically open. At first glance, you'll see the software is split visually, with the rack positioned along the top half of your screen and the sequencer across the bottom half. Notice the vertical navigation bar that runs along the upper right portion of the screen. By clicking and dragging up or down on this, you can reveal all of the current instruments and effects being utilized in the demo song as follows:

This is the hardware interface, which is followed by a fourteen-channel mixer, RV7000 Advanced Reverb, Kong Drum Designer, as well as the Dr. OctoRex Loop Player.

The sequencer is located in the bottom half of the screen and contains the track column on the left side and the MIDI clips positioned in an arrangement segment along the right side.

Understanding the Layout

To understand the basic operation of Reason, let's begin by focusing on each section of the demo song. The goal here is to become familiar with the different sections of the software, to be able to create a common dialog. As we move through the different tutorials, I will explain and elaborate on each section in greater detail. Let's start by examining the rack.

The Rack

Hardware Interface

The first object located in the rack is the Hardware Interface device. The purpose of this device is to act as the software equivalent of a physical sound card or the device that turns digital signals into an analog audio wave format. The Hardware Interface also allows usage of some of the more advanced MIDI features that will be discussed later in more detail. For starters, however, let's just focus on the audio portion of this feature.

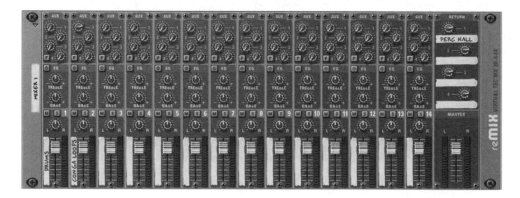

Note the Audio Input and Audio Output. These LED meters display visually which audio is being routed to each respective physical counterpart of the sound card. Built-in Output has already been selected by the active audio driver. My computer's default audio has two active audio inputs and two active audio outputs, therefore I see two red LEDs displayed underneath Audio Input 1 and 2. The illuminated LEDs are telling me that Audio Input 1 and 2 are currently active. The same can be said for the green LEDs located underneath Audio Output 1 and 2. If your audio interface contains sixteen inputs and sixteen outputs, all of the visible LEDs under each respective input and output would be illuminated.

The Mixer

Below the Hardware Interface, take note of the reMIX 14:2 mixer. A mixer is a device that allows for the blending of multiple streams of audio together to output them into a "stereo" pair, thereby allowing for all the parts to be combined.

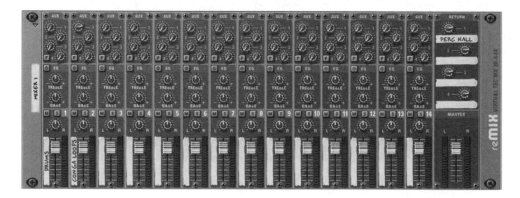

This particular mixer has the ability to blend fourteen mono and/or stereo sounds together. There's also a two-band equalizer, four aux sends, and four aux returns. You will also find volume faders and pan pots, as well as solo and mute buttons. This may seem like a lot of information to comprehend, but do not panic if you don't quite understand all the functions yet, as all will be clear as each is revealed in detail.

Instruments and Effects

Following the mixer is an RV7000 Advanced Reverb effects processor, as well as two instruments, a Kong Drum Designer and a Dr. OctoRex Loop Player.

Instruments and effects will be explained in greater detail in a later chapter, but for the time being, it's important to understand the basic signal flow of how the rack is wired. For starters, press the Tab key on your computer keyboard and let's have some fun.

I personally find this is one of the most amazing things about Reason. As you can see, the back of the rack is designed to allow you to visually understand the physical wiring of an actual audio rack. It is possible to trace the cables that are routed from your instruments and effects to see how they physically attach to the reMIX 14:2 mixer. First, note how the Kong is routed to Channel 1, while Dr. OctoRex is routed to Channel 2. The RV7000 is set up to receive input from Aux 1 and is routed back into the mixer via Return 1. The Master Out of the mixer is routed to Audio Output 1 and 2 on the Hardware Interface and allows you to hear all of the instruments and effects. These connect to the mixer, which then acts as the hub or nerve center of the software. This feature enables you to listen to each individual instrument routed to Audio Output 1 and 2. In the next section, you will look more closely at the sequencer.

The Sequencer

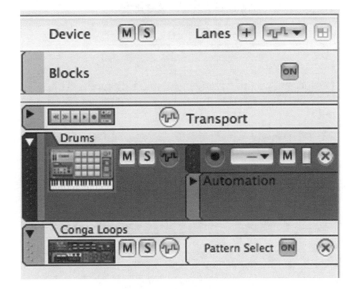

Just as with audio routing, this is the feature that enables you to record, edit, and play back MIDI data. The data is routed to specific tracks during recording. After the recording and subsequent editing, the playback of the data is routed to each respective instrument and effect, thereby triggering sounds that are, in turn, routed to the mixer and hardware interface, thus completing the entire signal flow.

Now you will take a closer look at some of the individual elements found on the sequencer page.

The two main sections of the sequencer page are the Track List and the Arrangement/Edit pane.

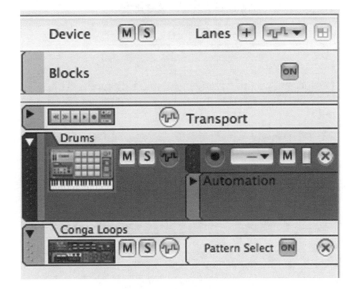

Track List

In the Track List, you'll find tracks that are dedicated to each instrument. When you create an instrument, a track is automatically created in the track column by default. Any device in Reason can be automated, but effects do not generate tracks in the track list by default. To automate effects, a track for the device must be manually created. In the example above, the Kong track has been selected, as identified by the dark gold color. The illuminated Rec

Ready red button lets Reason know that this is where the incoming MIDI data should be routed, recorded, and edited.

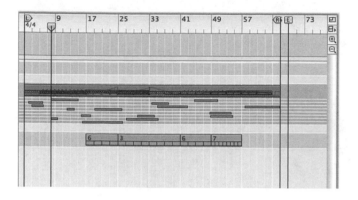

Arrangement/Edit Pane

To the right of the Track List is the Arrangement/Edit pane. In the example above, you see the Arrangement view of this window. Visible inside the pane is the MIDI note data, which appear in three parts visually. The first part appears as a solid gold clip; next are the automation data, which are represented as free-floating gold blocks for the Kong Drum Designer; and the third part appears as pattern automation, or a blue block, to represent the Dr. OctoRex.

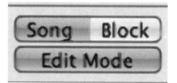

The upper left corner shows the Arrangement and Edit modes. (The arrangement mode called Block will be covered in full detail in the Advanced book.)

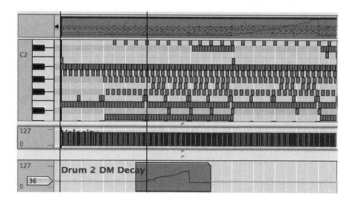

When Edit Mode is selected, the Arrangement/Edit pane switches over to enable the editing of individual notes, velocity, and automation data.

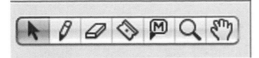

Tool Palette Tools

Tool Palette Tools allow you to create, edit, delete, and modify MIDI data.

Selector Tool

Selects one or more events for editing

Pencil Tool

Adds MIDI events or draws automation

Eraser Tool

Erases MIDI events and automation

Razor Tool

Splits MIDI events, clips, and automation

Mute Tool

Mutes individual notes, clips, and automation

Magnify Tool

Zooms in or out (To zoom out, press down the Option key.)

Hand Tool

Navigation tool

Another great feature of the Tool Palette Tools is the assignation of quick key commands, which can be used to quickly select each tool as needed. Press Q, W, E, R, T, Y, and U respectively to select each tool. This can be a great time-saver once you get accustomed to each command!

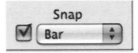

Snap

The Snap function forces any data to lock to a specific increment of time. In this case, Snap is set to Bar, which would cause any clip, note, or automation block to be move in one-measure increments. The options at which you can set this time to range from one bar to one sixty-fourth of a measure.

Inspector

The Inspector feature is like a window into any selected data on the Arrangement/Edit pane. In this particular instance, the clip starts at measure 8 and is seven measures long. The Inspector is incredibly useful for making sure all of the data is set in the desired position as well as duration. It will change depending on what type of clip or event is selected.

For instance, here's how the Inspector would read if you had selected an individual MIDI note. Notice that in addition to Position and Length, you see that Note and Velocity information is displayed as well.

Song Navigator

The Song Navigator is located between the Track and Arrangement/Edit and the Transport panes. This feature affords a bird's-eye view of the entire song.

Transport

The Transport is a global device that is always available for use whether you're looking at the rack or the sequencer. It is an extremely useful feature, not just for playback and recording; it also offers a whole host of necessary and useful functions described as follows.

In
Audio Input Meter

Out
Audio Output Meter

DSP (Digital Signal Processing)
This shows how much of your computer's processor is being used for the current function.

Calc (Calculation)
This displays activity when Reason is processing and/or loading samples.

Blocks
This is an advanced Arrangement tool that will be addressed more fully in the Advanced version. To disable, deselect the Blocks button.

Metronome
Provides a click track with Precount and Tap Tempo functionality.

Tempo
Calculated in beats per minute (bpm)

Time Signature
The default setting for this is 4/4.

Song Position
Displayed in two formats:
1. Musical (Bar . Beat . 16th Note . Tick) and
2. Time (hours:minutes:seconds:frames)

Transport Controls
Rewind / Fast Forward / Stop / Play / Record

Dub
New Take

Alt
Alternate Take

Q Rec
Quantize during Record

Left and Right Locators
These are used in conjunction with the bar ruler on the Arrangement/Edit pane and afford the ability to set up a loop for recording and editing.

Chapter 3

GETTING STARTED

Setting Preferences

In the last chapter, you were using the default demo song. For this tutorial, you will start with an empty rack. Before you begin, open up Reason's preferences and from General Preferences, select Empty Rack in the Song Start section.

Create a New Session

Now that you've set your song start preferences to Empty Rack, you can start a project from scratch. If you haven't done so already, initiate a new session by first opening the File menu and selecting New.

Once the new session is open, it should appear as an empty rack as shown here.

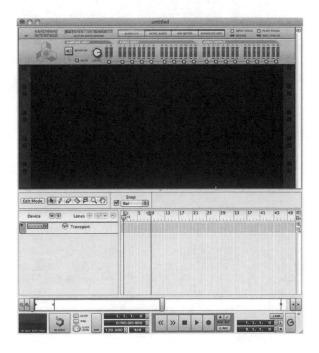

Save Your Session

Sometimes computers have a tendency to crash, so it is highly recommended to save your session periodically as you work. To do this, select Save from the File menu and name this session Chapter 3. As you proceed, try to develop the habit of saving periodically and often. The keyboard command for saving is Command + S.

Create a Mixer

Under the main menu options, select reMIX 14:2 from the Create menu. As a Reason specialist, I am often asked about the use of cabling in Reason and whether it is necessary to route the cables manually. I have found that Reason proves itself to be an intelligent application, provided you create, or establish, your procedure in the correct order. By your creating a mixer first, all instruments and effects will automatically route themselves to the next available mixer channel. However, should you prefer to do so manually, it is possible to bypass the default cabling, which will be covered in more detail in a later section.

Create a Dr. OctoRex Loop Player

After creating the mixer, next select Dr. OctoRex Loop Player from the Create menu. This will result in the configuration shown here.

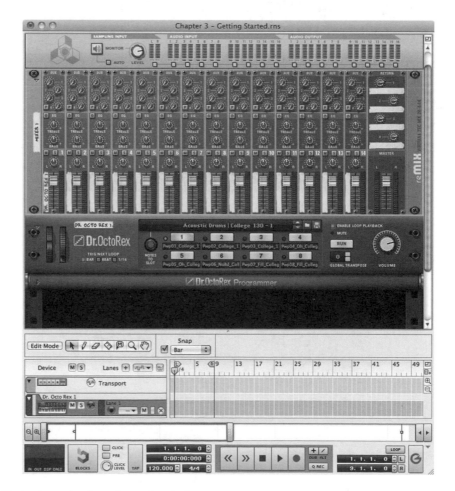

Notice how the first channel strip located to the left of the mixer "console tape" is now labeled Dr. OctoRex 1.

Next, click the Tab key to view the cabling.

Note how Main Output of the Dr. OctoRex is now connected to Channel 1 Inputs Left and Right.

Also confirm that Master Out of the mixer is now connected to Audio Outputs 1 and 2 of Audio I/O on the Hardware Interface.

Working with the Dr. OctoRex Loop Player

Let's become acquainted with the Dr. OctoRex.

Click the Run button.

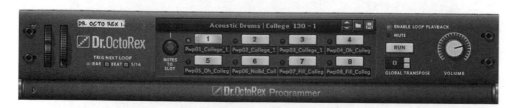

Dr. OctoRex is a loop playback device that allows for up to eight different loops to be loaded and played back simultaneously. By default, the instrument is loaded with a preset of sounds. The default preset is called Acoustic Drums / College 130–1.

With the Run button engaged, you should be able to listen to Slot 1. Feel free to explore the different variations of loops loaded into each of the other seven slots. Note how each slot is labeled with the name of each individual loop that is the preset. Slots 1 through 6 contain different variations of drum loops, while Slots 7 through 8 are set up to contain fills.

Now, let's explore several different presets.

Using the Browse Patch Button

Select Browse Patch and navigate to Drums >Electronic Drums > Bomb Squad > Bomb Squad Beats 80–89 bpm.

Dr. OctoRex should now display Bomb Squad Beats 80–89 bpm and have six loops loaded into each respective slot.

Select one of the Bomb Squad loops and hit the Run button again.

Now, try to evaluate the sound you hear. Do you notice that it seems little too fast?

This is because the patch has a tempo range of 80–89 bpm (beats per minute). Now try changing the tempo of the session to better match the tempo range of 80–89 bpm made by the Dr. OctoRex. To do so, double-click on the Tempo section of the Transport window and input 85, and press Enter.

Next, try clicking Run again on the Dr. OctoRex. You will note that this time it sounds more appropriate.

Importing a Loop

Another useful option afforded by the Dr. OctoRex is ability to import individual loops into the slots. This allows for creating your own patch with custom-loaded loops. In the previous section, when you used the Browse Patch function and selected the Bomb Squad patch, you were telling Reason to load a collection of loops, and in this case, six loops were loaded.

Select the blank title box beneath the Slot 7 button. You will see a text bubble appear, from which you should select Open Browser.

In the File browser window, under Locations and Favorites, select Reason Factory Sound Bank.

Navigate to Dr. OctoRex Instrument Loops > Bomb Squad > BSQ_DestructionVox_092. rx2.

The newly selected DestructionVox loop is now loaded into Slot 7 of your Dr. OctoRex Loop Player.

Let's leave the Dr. OctoRex like this for now and proceed to load up a new instrument.

Create a Subtractor

Select Subtractor from the Create drop-down menu.

The Subtractor should appear underneath the Dr. OctoRex Loop Player. Also, notice the label next to Channel 2 on reMIX 14:2, which will now read Subtractor 1.

Select the Tab key to see the routing of the Subtractor to the mixer. The "main" audio output is routed to the Left/Mono input of Channel 2 on the mixer.

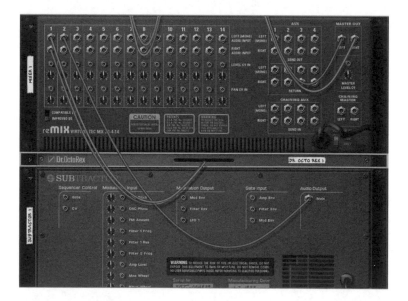

Select Tab again to see the front side of this rack.

Now you should go ahead and play some notes on your MIDI keyboard controller. The sound you will hear is the default Bass Guitar patch.

Browse Subtractor Patches

Select the Browse Patch button on the Subtractor. The Patch Browser window will open to reveal all categories of the patches available for use in the Subtractor synthesizer.

	Patch Browser: SubTractor 1		
Search in:	Local disks	Search For:	Find
	Subtractor Patches	Show: All Instruments	
Locations and Favorites	Name	Modified	Size
Desktop	Lesko Deep.zyp	Jun 30, 2010 6:04 AM	1 kB
grandpoohbah	MatrixBass2.zyp	Jun 30, 2010 6:04 AM	1 kB
Documents	Mitsubishi.zyp	Jun 30, 2010 6:04 AM	1 kB
Reason Folder	MK5 Fivdee.zyp	Jun 30, 2010 6:04 AM	1 kB
Recent Patches	Muddy Bass.zyp	Jun 30, 2010 6:04 AM	1 kB
	Nitrobass.zyp	Jun 30, 2010 6:04 AM	1 kB
Reason Factory Sound Bank	Picked bass.zyp	Jun 30, 2010 6:04 AM	1 kB
Orkester Sound Bank	Plastic.zyp	Jun 30, 2010 6:04 AM	1 kB
Showcase	Polka Tuba.zyp	Jun 30, 2010 6:04 AM	1 kB
Epic Poly.thor	Punch Bass.zyp	Jun 30, 2010 6:04 AM	1 kB
New Favorites List	PylonBass.zyp	Jun 30, 2010 6:04 AM	1 kB
	Raw Hip Hop Bass.zyp	Jun 30, 2010 6:04 AM	1 kB
	ResonBass.zyp	Jun 30, 2010 6:04 AM	1 kB
	Reverse Bass.zyp	Jun 30, 2010 6:04 AM	1 kB
	RhombusBass.zyp	Jun 30, 2010 6:04 AM	1 kB
	RnB Bass.zyp	Jun 30, 2010 6:04 AM	1 kB
	Search Bass.zyp	Jun 30, 2010 6:04 AM	1 kB
	SlangBass.zyp	Jun 30, 2010 6:04 AM	1 kB
	Standarlogue.zyp	Jun 30, 2010 6:04 AM	1 kB

Info	Details	Audition
	Patch Type: SubTractor	Play ☑ Autoplay
Factory Sound Bank		
Reason Factory Sound Bank © 2010 Propellerhead Software AB, Sweden		▲ Select Previous ▼ Select Next
		Loading
?		Cancel OK

Select Bass and explore some of the different bass sounds the Subtractor provides.

An alternate method for quickly selecting patches is to use the Next/Previous Patch button located to the left of the Browse Patch button.

By selecting the top or bottom triangle, you will move either forward or backward within the Bass Patch folder of the Subtractor.

Once you are finished exploring some of the bass sounds of the Subtractor, be sure return to the Punch Bass patch selection.

In the next chapter, you will explore how to record MIDI using Reason.

Chapter 4
RECORDING

Selecting a Track

The very first step you should always take when starting a recording session is to confirm that you have selected the correct track. This refers back to the concept of signal flow and knowing where to route the incoming MIDI data that's being triggered by your MIDI controller.

On the sequencer rack, select the Subtractor track.

Notice how the background color of the selected track has changed to a darker shade. Furthermore, note there is now a red border highlighting the Synth icon, which resembles a miniature version of the Subtractor. This is an indication that the Master Keyboard selection is now set up within Preferences. Also take note of how two of the displayed buttons are now red. Your focus will be the red button containing the solid black circle inside, or the Record Ready button. To simplify the track selection process, first select the Master Keyboard input so that you only need to select the desired track for Reason to know where the MIDI data is to be routed for recording.

Now play a few notes using your MIDI keyboard. You will hear the Subtractor playing the Punch Bass patch you selected and set in the previous chapter.

Now you are ready to set up a metronome, but before doing so, first mute the Dr. OctoRex track by selecting the square M button displayed with this track.

The Metronome

Setting up a metronome is a great way to work when producing music because it provides a timing reference that is very useful in the editing and arranging processes. If you record a MIDI section without a timing reference, it is highly likely that the bar ruler will not match the recording, which makes the editing and arranging process more difficult.

For example, pretend you are recording a one-measure MIDI clip with a tempo of 160 bpm. If the Reason sequencer tempo is set to 120 bpm, the result would manifest as a MIDI section that doesn't match the tempo of your bar ruler. This would then render the Snap function useless in editing, due to the mismatched timing.

Now, let's take a closer look at the metronome and its settings.

On the Transport window located at the bottom of the screen, use the Click button to engage the metronome. Notice there is a higher-pitched sound on the first beat of every measure, followed by three sound beats at a slightly lower pitch. Note the Time Signature section on the Transport window, which is set by default to 4/4 time. The first number shown is equivalent to the first beat (or the higher-pitched sound) followed by the three beats at the lower pitch. This can be adjusted by changing the time signature to 3/4 time so that the metronome only cycles through three beats instead of four, with the first beat as the higher-pitched sound, followed by only two beats at the lower pitch. For the purposes of this tutorial, you will be working in 4/4 time, so be sure to return the setting to this.

Next, engage the Pre button located under the Click button in the Metronome section.

The Pre button engages the function Precount, which is essentially a count-off that occurs before recording begins. This is quite helpful because it allows you to hear the tempo at which you will be recording just prior to starting the recording session. By default, this is set to run for one measure; however, you can easily modify the length of the Precount by selecting Options under the main menu and navigating to Number of Precount Bars to select either 1, 2, 3, or 4 as possible settings.

Now, select 2, to set Precount to last for two bars (eight beats) before recording begins.

If you determine that the metronome is either too loud or not loud enough, you can easily modify the volume adjusting the Click Level knob.

Now you are ready to record a MIDI section.

Recording MIDI

From the Transport window, click the square red Record button or simply use the quick keyboard command Command + Return.

Now, using your MIDI instrument, play a few bars while making an effort to maintain time with the tempo set by the metronome. When you have finished playing this section, simply tap the spacebar to stop recording.

Congratulations! You've just created your first recording in Reason.

You will find a MIDI clip is now visible inside the arrangement window.

To return to the beginning of the newly recorded section, click the Stop button in the Transport window or simply use the quick keyboard command Shift + Return to perform the same function.

Now, when you press Play or tap the spacebar, you can listen to your recording.

This not the only method that can be used to maintain time with tempo, so here I will introduce another method that you may prefer to use instead. I personally find using a metronome feels less organic than using drum loops, which are my preferred method of maintaining time with tempo.

Let's give using drum loops a try. Simply press the Mute button on the Dr. OctoRex Loop Player and first listen to the MIDI recording you just made with the Dr. OctoRex loop playing together with your recording. The results of your recording might match the drum loop fine, but if not, you will want to rerecord the Subtractor track using this loop instead of the metronome. To do so, first select the MIDI clip on the Arrangement pane and select Delete on your computer keyboard to clear the data.

Now, use your instrument to record a new MIDI clip using the Dr. OctoRex loop, instead of the metronome, to maintain timing. Make sure you have deselected the Click button on the Transport window to disengage the metronome and allow the Dr. OctoRex loop to provide the timing reference. I recommend keeping the Pre button engaged, as this will give you the desired Precount you previously set before recording.

Now let's focus on how to record MIDI with the Dr. OctoRex loop. First, be sure to mute the Subtractor track, leaving only the Dr. OctoRex track selected.

There are two methods of working with MIDI and the Dr. OctoRex Loop Player. The first is Recording Patterns and the second is Copy Loop to Track.

Recording Patterns

Begin by selecting Slot 4 and press Record on the Transport window (or press the Record keyboard command). After the song position pointer moves two bars, select Slot 6, and then toggle between Slots 4 and 6 every two bars until the song position pointer reaches measure 9.

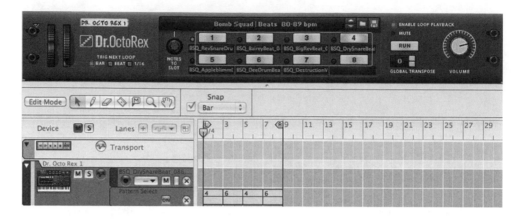

Notice the appearance of a new lane, which is labeled Pattern Select and displays the graphical representation of each selected slot. Also note the green outline that now appears around the Slot Selection section of the Dr. OctoRex loop. This green box denotes that this particular section has been automated.

Double click the Stop button on the transport (or press Shift + Return) to move the song position pointer back to the beginning of the arrangement, and then press Play. Observe how the patterns will now automatically switch between Slots 4 and 6 every two measures. This is the first method that can be utilized as a recording pattern.

Copy Loop to Track

While the previous method works fine for recording patterns, I find this next method, Copy Loop to Track, to be more useful when making more complex arrangements, so let's give this method a try.

First turn your attention to the Bar Ruler located at the top of the sequencer window.

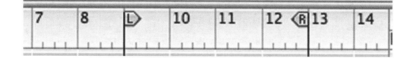

Use the mouse to click and grab the right locator, labeled R, and move it to Measure 13. Next, grab the left locator, labeled L, and move it to Measure 9.

Now select Slot 4 on the Dr. OctoRex Loop Player. To open or unfold the Dr. OctoRex Programmer, select the triangle in the upper left corner of the programmer window located just below the main Dr. OctoRex window, to expand this window fully as shown.

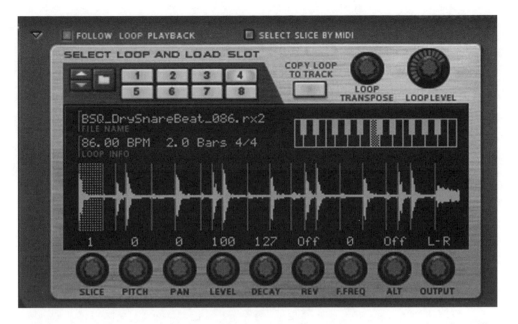

This will reveal the full Dr. OctoRex Programmer window. On the left side of this programmer, you will see the Select Loop and Load Slot box, which is outlined in silver. In the upper middle section of this box, locate the button labeled Copy Loop to Track and click it.

Now, in the Arrangement pane of the sequencer section, you will see two MIDI clips placed in between the four bar selection framed by the L (left) and R (right) locators. This shows the MIDI data to be extracted from Loop 4 of the Dr. OctoRex loop. Notice how with this method, as compared to the previous one, you are able to manually edit each individual slice of the drum loop being used. This will be further explored in the next chapter as we cover the MIDI editing process, as well as examine in more detail the various editors available.

Chapter 5
EDITING MIDI

In the last chapter, you explored various methods for recording MIDI data, and further, created a data file. Now let's a look at how to edit the data you have just created. Reason contains three types of editors; Key, Drum, and Slice, and it is possible to view MIDI data using any of the three editors, regardless of the instrument in use. However, the instrument being used will determine which of the three different edit modes will be engaged during the editing process. Let's begin by focusing on the use of the Key editor, as this is the editor used by the majority of instruments.

Key Editor

The first step is to mute the Dr. OctoRex track and unmute the Subtractor track. There are two ways to engage the MIDI editor; however, either of these methods will result in the same outcome.

Select the Edit button in the upper left corner of the sequencer page to change the view from Arrangement to Edit. Or you can simply double-click directly on the clip of MIDI data you will be editing.

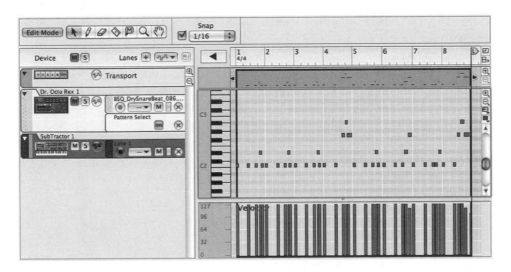

This image shows the view of the Subtractor track with the MIDI clip selected. The blue bar at the top is the similar to the view of the clip in the Arrangement view. Just below that is the aforementioned Key Editor. Note the vertical keyboard displayed along the left side of the editor. The MIDI note events (in small red blocks) appear in the range of C2 on the keyboard. At the very top you will find a bar ruler, which displays this MIDI clip as a total of eight bars in length.

Let's zoom in for a closer look at the data. To do this, first select the Magnify tool (quick key command Y) and select the notes within the first measure. Another way to engage the zoom function is to repeatedly click the H key until the desired level of zoom has been reached.

In the figure above, take note of the five notes displayed in Measure 1. Note how the second note is slightly darker and has a small triangle displayed to the right side of the red block. This indicates that this note has been selected for editing. The Inspector section at the top of the editor displays detailed information about the selected note.

To move a note, simply select and hold your mouse or track pad and move the note to the desired position. Other edit functions include Copy, Cut, and Paste. This can also be achieved by selecting each function from the main Edit menu or by right-clicking on the mouse.

A faster and easier method of copying or duplicating a note is the Option + Drag method. To execute this, simply press and hold the Option key while simultaneously selecting and then moving the "note" to the desired position. Notice the green + symbol that appears when using this function. Make sure you release the Option key last to complete the operation, otherwise you'll end up moving the note without copying it.

A quick way to remove unwanted data is to select the information to be deleted and press the Delete key on your computer keyboard. This will remove the data and you can resume editing if desired.

Sequencer Tools

Let's explore the sequencer tools that are available in the "floating" tool window. You will find many of these tools useful when editing data.

First, look at the Main menu and select Window > Show Tool Window, or press F8 to engage the device palette in the default window of the Show Tool window. This allows you to create any device available in Reason and offers a quick way of adding any device from the Create drop-down from the Main menu. Now select the Wrench/Screwdriver icon at the top of the Tool window to then select Sequencer Tools.

All of the functions of the Sequencer Tools window are available for both individual notes and entire MIDI clips (from within the Arrangement pane).

Quantize

The most commonly used function is found in the Quantize Notes section. Quantization is a method of time correction in which the start positions of selected note data are automatically aligned to a predefined, absolute grid. By default, the Quantization value is set to 1/16.

Let's start by selecting all the notes in Measure 1. The easiest way to do this is by "rubber-band" selecting. To execute this, start by clicking and holding down your mouse/track pad while selecting all the notes that appear within Measure 1. You'll notice a rectangular box will appear and all the notes within this box are selected.

An alternative to this method is to simply Shift + Click each note individually. Do this by holding down the Shift key on your computer keyboard while individually selecting each note by clicking on it with your mouse.

Once you have selected all the notes in Measure 1, click the Apply button under the Quantize section of Sequencer Tools to engage the quantization function.

Pay close attention to the selected notes. They will be moved automatically into position, or quantized, to the nearest sixteenth note. A great way to compare this to your previously recorded performance is to then analyze the notes using the information displayed in the Inspector.

Transpose

Another useful function of the Sequencer Tools window is the Transpose Notes section. Set the Transpose Notes value to the setting –12 semitones to move all the current notes down one full octave in position. With all the notes in Measure 1 selected, next click the Apply button.

Notice how all the selected notes are moved down one full octave. The note range of the MIDI data has moved from the previous range of C2 down to C1.

There are many other Sequencer Tools functions that you will explore in greater depth in the "Creating an Arrangement" chapter later in this book. However, there is one more editing function to cover here.

Velocity

The final editing function that I'd like to focus on introducing is the editing of velocity. The definition of velocity is "The speed of something in a given direction." In musical terms, it's often equated to how hard you pressed the keys of your MIDI controller that, in turn, controls the volume. (Velocity can be utilized to control any number of sound functions, as we'll explore in more detail later.)

Notice at the bottom of the Key Editor pane is a box labeled Velocity. Here you see a series of vertical bars aligned with the start position of each note displayed in the Key Editor pane. The range of data is designated from 0 to 127 (0 = 0% to 127 = 100%). As you can see in the previous graphical examples, the velocity is set at 127.

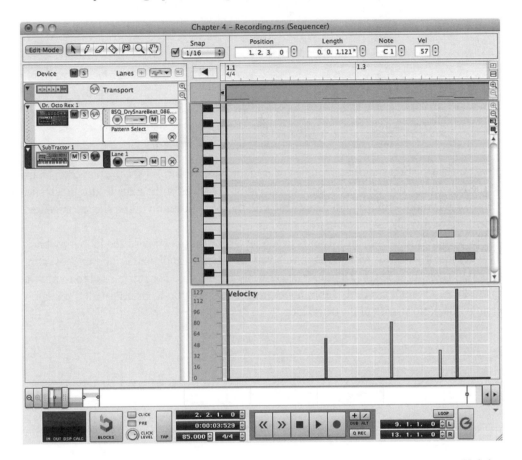

If you wish to edit this data, you can make adjustments from the Inspector (Vel) by clicking in the Vel box and entering a value. Another method is to select the Pencil Tool (key command W) from the Tool Palette tools and use it to draw in the desired values. Notice how the notes with different velocities are displayed in different colors.

Now that we have covered the main editing tools, let's take a look at the MIDI data generated by the Dr. OctoRex Loop Player.

Mute the Subtractor track and unmute the Dr. OctoRex track. You may have to navigate to Measure 9, where you previously placed the MIDI clip when using the Copy Loop to Track function on the Dr. OctoRex track.

Slice Editor

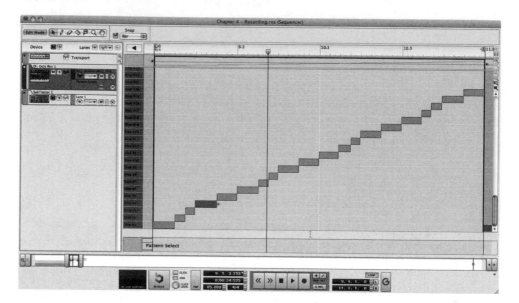

Here you see the Edit pane has switched over to the Slice Editor. Where the piano keyboard of the Key Editor had been, now you see displayed the slices of the Slice Editor. Each slice of the loop is represented a midi note event with the exact duration of the slice represented. There are twenty slices shown in this loop.

Place your cursor over Slice 1 and click. You'll hear that portion of the loop play back. The genius of working with loops in this way is you have independent control over the sound of each slice. The MIDI notes can be easily reconfigured or rerecorded to remix the drum loop. This is incredibly flexible because it enables you to dramatically yet easily change the performance of the drum loop.

Chapter 6
THE REASON DEVICES

Instruments

Reason comes complete with eight fantastic-sounding instruments to use in your music production. These instruments are broken down into three categories: synthesizers, samplers, and drum machines. Let's first take a tour of each instrument and get an idea of what each kind of sounds has to offer. In this First QuickBook Pro book, we will focus on using the presets and obtaining a basic and functional understanding of the types of sounds each instrument is best suited for providing. After this, I recommend you follow up with the Second QuickBook Pro book for more extensive explanations of the detailed functions of the instruments and their specific use, to achieve an advanced understanding.

Synthesizers

Reason ships with three synthesizers included. They are called the Subtractor Analog Synthesizer, the Malstrom Graintable Synthesizer and the Thor Polysonic Synthesizer.

Subtractor Analog Synthesizer

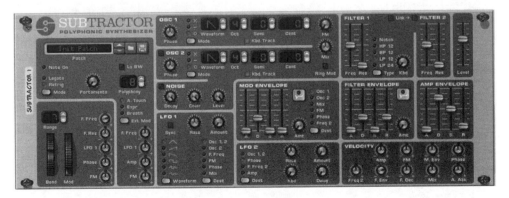

The Subtractor Analog Synthesizer is a polyphonic synthesizer based on analog subtractive synthesis. It has two oscillators, two filters, three envelopes, and two LFOs.

The types of sounds produced by this synthesizer are essentially the same ones found on any analog synthesizer you may be familiar with using. It's great for creating any type of synthesizer sound possible. The same is true of the Synth Basses, Pads, Leads, FX, and Synth Percussion features. It's a great all-around synthesizer as its programming is straightforward, thereby making it quite easy to use.

Malstrom Graintable Synthesizer

The Malstrom is a completely new type of synthesizer that combines both granular and wavetable synthesis to produce unique sounds that are nothing short of stellar.

Granular synthesis is accomplished by generating a number of short contiguous grains (or segments) of sounds. These segments are modified by changing the order and properties of the grains, resulting in a variety of dynamic sounds that are very complex and often unusual.

Wavetable synthesis is the precursor to the sampler and uses short recorded sounds arranged into oscillator banks. The banks of sampled waveforms are selected and processed through typical sound-shaping modules such as filters, envelopes, and LFOs. One unique property of wavetable synthesis is the ability to sweep through the bank of sampled waveforms, creating unique "garbled" effect.

The result of combining these two types of synthesis affords the ability to produce sounds that are virtually unobtainable by any other synthesizer in either hardware or software form.

The preset categories include Synth Bass, Pads, Monosynths, Polysynths, FX, Percussion, and Rhythmic. You can expect an array of swirling, metallic, sharp, aggressive, and distorted sounds.

Thor Polysonic Synthesizer

The Thor Polysonic synthesizer is based on the concept of a semimodular synthesizer. This approach provides the ultimate in flexibility with the ability to change to different modules, each offering a different sound creation, or processing, capability.

There are three oscillators, each having six options to choose from when using this synthesizer: Analog, Wavetable, Phase Modulation, FM Pair, Multi Oscillator, and Noise. The filter section offers three filters with four options to choose from, including Low Pass, Variable State, Comb, and Formant. Additionally, three envelopes, two LFOs, and an FX section round out the sound manipulation palette. An extensive routing matrix and a built-in step sequencer bring this instrument to a new level of sound-creation capability. The sounds range from Synth Bass, Pad, Lead, Choir/Vocal, Sequenced, Rhythmic, Percussion, FX, and Textures.

Digital Samplers

NN19 Digital Sampler

The NN19 Digital Sampler is an instrument not unlike a synthesizer. Instead of using an analog oscillator, a sampler uses prerecorded audio files to generate sounds. Beyond that, all the basic synthesizer controls are available to shape and manipulate the desired sound. Samplers are excellent for creating organic sounds because they use the waveforms instead of only trying to synthesize them. If you are looking for any combination of piano, guitar, violin, acoustic drums, and/or percussion effects, then this is the instrument for you. Categories of sounds include: Bass, Brass, and Woodwinds, Guitar, Mallet and Ethnic, Organ, Piano, Strings, Synth and Keyboard, Raw Synth Waveforms, and Voice.

NN-XT Advanced Sampler

The NN-XT Advanced Sampler is very much like the NN19 Sampler but has some additional features that give it greater expression. It allows for a more complex setup with sophisticated layering and velocity switching. Other features include the ability to load sound fonts, and eight stereo outs. This instrument also ships with its own dedicated sound library that focuses on orchestral sounds. This impressive sound bank includes Brass, Woodwinds, Strings, Orchestral Percussion, Harp, and Mallet sounds in its repertoire. While it's more complex in its setup and custom sound creation, the expressiveness it provides is second to none.

Drum Machines

Dr. OctoRex Loop Player

The Dr. OctoRex Loop Player is the new and improved version of the Dr. Rex Loop Player. It adds the ability to load and play back up to eight loops simultaneously in an extremely flexible and creative way. The Dr. OctoRex plays Rex files, which are files processed by a separate utility program called Recycle. Recycle analyzes drum and instrument loops and processes the data in a way that slices each individual drum hit or sound based on transient of the sound. Slicing the loop in this manner allows you to change the tempo of the loop without changing the pitch or processing with time compression/expansion, a process with artifacts that often cause changes the feeling of the loop. The addition of synthesizer controls and the ability to adjust various parameters per slice really make this instrument stand out in terms of functionality.

ReDrum Drum Computer

ReDrum Drum Computer is a drum machine based on the vintage design of the Roland TR-808 and TR-909 machines created in the early to mid-1980s. It boasts ten individual slots for loading complete kits and individual sounds. It even lets you sample directly into each slot with just a simple click of a button. Other features include pitch and tone adjustment, level and pan controls; also, each of the ten slots has individual outputs, which make mixing and process a breeze. The sequencer section offers four banks of eight patterns for a total of thirty-two patterns per instrument. It also has the ability to "copy pattern to track," which is really useful when building and editing an arrangement.

Kong Drum Designer

The Kong Drum Designer is an instrument capable of a multitude of functions beyond just making drum sounds. The initial concept allows for various types of modeling and sample playback options, including NN Nano Sampler, Nurse Rex Loop Player, Physical Bass Drum, Physical Snare Drum, Physical Tom Tom, Synth Bass Drum, Synth Snare Drum, Synth High Hat and Synth Tom Tom. Other features include a Multiple Effects processor dedicated to each drum pad, as well as Bus and Master Effects. Another added feature is the ability to route sounds through the instrument, allowing the Kong to be used just like an FX processor.

Effects Processors

Signal Processors

Signal processors are typically used as an "insert" effect. The audio signal is routed into the effect, processed, and passed on to the mixer. This is commonly used when the processed output signal has replaced the original sound from the instrument.

Equalization

– PEQ-2–Two Band Parametric EQ (Equalizer)

The PEQ-2 is a two-band parametric EQ, or equalizer. The function of an equalizer is to correct imbalances within the audio frequency spectrum. Each band of the EQ has a Frequency, Q, and Gain control that can be used to make adjustments.

Dynamic Processor

– Comp-01–Auto Makeup Gain Compressor

The Comp-01 is a compressor/limiter that is used to control the dynamics (or amplitude) of a sound by making louder sounds softer and softer sounds louder. The overall processed signal is more even and often results in individual instruments with more presence and longer sustain. The interface includes Ratio, Threshold, Attack, Release, and Gain Meter.

Distortion

– D-11 Foldback Distortion

The D-11 provides the typical array of distortion effects and is extremely simple and versatile to use. Controls include adjustable Amount and Foldback settings.

– Scream 4–Sound Destruction Unit

The Scream 4 is a sonic destruction unit that provides a vast array of distortion effects including analog, digital, tape emulation, and ring modulation. Controls include Damage Control, Distortion Type with two parameter knobs, a three-band EQ, and a "body" circuit that emulates different cabinet types. From subtle tape compression to the sound of a fully blown speaker, this effect processor will inspire you to create extraordinary sounds.

Phase

– PH-90 Phaser

The PH-90 is a classic phaser-effect production unit that shifts portions of audio out of phase and mixes it back in with the original signal, causing a sweeping sound. This is a typical guitar or pad effect that creates movement in the sound.

Controls include Frequency, Split, Width, Rate, and Frequency Modulation (including tempo synchronization), as well as Feedback.

Time-Based Effects

Time-based effects are often used in conjunction with auxiliary sends on a mixer. This type of effect is best employed with a mix of both the original, or "Dry," signal and the processed, or "Wet," signal. When using the effects via the auxiliary sends, the effect processors will automatically be set to fully Wet. It is possible to use time-based effects such as Insert effects. When this method is engaged, you can use the Dry/Wet knob to balance the processed and unprocessed signal to your desired taste.

Reverb

– RV7000 Advanced Reverb

The RV7000 Advanced Reverb is a high-quality reverb with nine algorithms ranging from rooms and halls to echoes and special effects. The palette of available presets is vast, but additional editing can also be accomplished by utilizing the Remote Programmer. Furthermore, there is also an EQ and Gate section that allows you to dial in your sound with even greater control.

– RV-7 Digital Reverb

The RV-7 Digital Reverb is a simple yet effective reverb with algorithms ranging from rooms to halls and special effects such as echo and gate. One the desired algorithm has been chosen, you can quickly tailor your sound with the Size, Decay, Damp, and Dry/Wet control settings.

Delay

– DDL-1 Digital Delay Line

The DDL-1 Digital Delay Line is a monophonic delay (with stereo output) that allows for the programming of precision delay lines. It can also be synchronized with the Reason sequencer with up to sixteen steps at various set lengths. The unit can be configured to work in "free" mode, with parameters set to work in milliseconds. Feedback, Pan, and Dry/Wet round out the controls in this simple yet fun effects processor.

Chorus/Flanger

– CF-101

The CF-101 Chorus/Flanger creates a combined chorus/flange effect. It's a typical effect used to create movement and motion by delaying small amounts of signal and modulating the rate of the built in LFO. The controls include Delay and Feedback, as well as Rate and Modulation amounts (with sequencer synchronization). The unit also features a Send mode, which sets the unit to either Insert or Aux Send mode.

Unison

– UN-16

The UN-16 is a device that emulates the Unison mode on a synthesizer, which provides an effect of multiple voices slightly detuned. Copying the incoming signal and then slightly delaying and pitching the individual voices create this effect. The unit has settings of four, eight, and sixteen voices with Detune and Dry/Wet controls.

Filter Effects

Envelope Controlled Filter

– ECF-42

The ECF-42 Envelope Controlled Filter is a multimode resonant filter designed to create envelope effects. It features 3 filter types: 12 dB Band Pass, 12 dB Low Pass, and 24 dB Low Pass. The unit is designed to work with pattern devices or can otherwise be triggered with a MIDI signal. Controls include Frequency Cutoff, Resonance, Envelope Amount, Velocity, and standard envelope controls (including Attack, Decay, Sustain, and Release).

Digital Vocoder

- BV512 Digital Vocoder

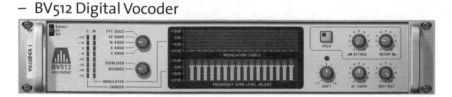

The BV512 Digital Vocoder is a fantastic sound-manipulation tool. By using two different instruments or sound inputs (Modulator and Carrier), you can create a number of effects, including FFT Equalization and talking drums or synthesizers. The famous "robot voice" effect can be easily achieved by using this device. It features five different modes ranging from 4 to 512 bands. Controls include Band Selection, Equalizer/Vocoder Mode, Modulation Levels, Frequency Band Levels Adjustment, Hold, Attack, Decay, Frequency Shift, High Frequency Emphasis, and Dry/Wet controls.

M-Class Effects

M-Class Equalizer

The M-Class Equalizer is a mastering-grade equalizer that features two bands of parametric equalization, two bands of shelf equalization (High and Low) and a Low Cut Filter that removes frequencies below 30 Hz. The unit features a graphic window that shows frequency curves and displays controls for Frequency, Gain, and Q settings. The unit is designed to be a mastering equalizer on the stereo bus of the mixer, but is also extremely effective at equalizing frequencies of single instruments.

M-Class Stereo Imager

The M-Class Stereo Imager is a dual-band stereo processor that splits the signal into two frequency bands and allows for discrete control over the perception of width of both the High and Low frequency bands. This is a fantastic unit to use for focusing low frequencies while widening high-frequency content.

M-Class Compressor

The M-Class Compressor is a stereo compressor featuring side-chain input. Not unlike the Comp-01 compressor that controls dynamics and the perception of loudness, the M-Class Compressor adds some fantastic features, including a soft knee setting, side-chain input, and adaptive release. The side-chain input can be used for ducking effects and de-essing when used in conjunction together with an equalizer. The adaptive release allows for more transparent sound in your production.

M-Class Maximizer

The M-Class Maximizer is a "look-ahead" limiter that allows for the maximization of sound levels without digital clipping. The look-ahead function gives a four-millisecond period of time, so the device is able to see into the future and prevent signal amplitudes from exceeding 0 dB. The unit also features a soft clip option, which not only prevents digital clipping but also introduces a warm, harmonic distortion.

Utility Devices

Merger and Splitter

Spider Audio Merger and Splitter

The Spider Audio Merger and Splitter is a device that allows for the merging or splitting of audio signals. The unit features four stereo inputs to a single stereo output. This function is not unlike a mixer, but it contains no Gain or Pan controls. It also has the ability to split a stereo input into four separate stereo outputs, making this a superior utility used to great effect for advanced routing capabilities.

Spider CV Merger and Splitter

The Spider CV Merger and Splitter is a device that allows for the merging or splitting of CV (Control Voltage) and Gate signals. The unit features four CV/Gate inputs to one CV/Gate output. It also has two single CV/Gate inputs to four CV/Gate output. For added flexibility, one of the split signals (Inv) is inverted, allowing for the inversion of the incoming signal. This is a great utility for routing a pattern generator to multiple devices. It also aids in the creation of complex LFOs.

Pattern Generators

Matrix Analog Pattern Sequencer

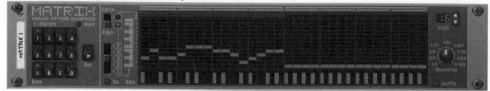

The Matrix Analog Pattern Sequencer is a pattern generator. It does not create sounds on its own, but when cabled to a synthesizer, the unit produces CV (pitch) and Gate (note on/ off with velocity). It also has a separate CV Curve output that allows for sequencing CV used for creating CV curves with any CV input on a synthesizer or effects device. The Pattern Sequencer features four banks of eight patterns for a total of thirty-two patterns per device. Each pattern can have up to thirty-two steps at resolutions ranging from half to 1/128 notes and has the ability to shuffle or swing notes. The CV and Gate are programmed on the Keys interface and offer a full one-octave view, with a range of up to five octaves that can be switched using the Octave switch located at the left of the device. Each horizontal block represents a note (as noted on the vertical keyboard to the left of the device). At the bottom of the unit, you'll see the Gate section. It features vertical blocks that may be resized, which will affect velocity output. When no vertical block is present, the blank slot acts as a rest.

RPG-8 Monophonic Arpeggiator

The RPG-8 Monophonic Arpeggiator is a pattern generator. This device does not generate sounds on its own, but acts as a MIDI to CV converter. The unit generates patterns, or arpeggios, by playing notes or chords on your MIDI keyboard controller that, in turn, are converted to Note CV and Gate signals used to generate patterns. The Arpeggiator features several pattern styles including Up, Up-Down, Down, Random, and Manual. It allows for arpeggiated patterns from one to four octaves and an insert section adds variations to the patterns, with a resolution of one measure to 1/128 notes with synchronization or free running. It also allows for the scaling of the gate signal. To the right of the unit is a pattern editor, which allows for even more control and flexibility with the added ability to introduce rests into the arpeggiated pattern. On the left side of the unit, the device also features velocity control. This allows for fixed velocities, or when in Manual mode, will pass through the incoming velocity generated by your MIDI keyboard controller. The device shines as a performance tool with the ability to create patterns on the fly with superior results. And if you are a novice keyboard player, this can be your secret weapon!

Reason Rebirth Input Machine

The ReBirth input machine is a device that allows you to connect Propellerheads Rebirth to Reason. ReBirth was the precursor to Reason and featured two TB303s, a TR-808 Drum Machine, and a TR-909 Drum Machine. ReBirth was a fantastic software for creating electronic music, but it is currently discontinued and only available for use on the PC. However, it will also be offered as application for the iPhone.

Mixers

reMIX 14:2 Mixer

The reMIX 14:2 is a stereo mixing device that allows for the merging of up to fourteen stereo or mono signals into a stereo output. Each channel features a Volume Fader, Pan Pot, Mute and Solo buttons, two-band High and Low Shelf Equalizers, and four Auxiliary sends. The Master section displayed on the left contains four dedicated auxiliary returns and a Stereo Master Fader to control the overall output of the session. This device serves as the nerve center because all devices are connected to and mixed when you are using it. It is possible to chain several mixers together to obtain higher track counts with in your session.

Line Mixer 6:2

The Line Mixer 6:2 is a mixing device that features six stereo inputs and one stereo output. Each input module on the mixer features a Volume Pot, Pan Pot, Mute and Solo buttons, and a singe Auxiliary send.

The Master section features a Master Volume knob for controlling the overall volume of mixed signals and a dedicated Auxiliary return. This is a great mixer for connecting a number of instruments together to create a "submix."

The Combinator

The Combinator is a unique device that allows for multiple instruments, effects, pattern generators, mixers, and so forth, to be nested inside it. This "nesting" of devices allows for extremely complex routing capabilities that can be saved and recalled at will: a huge time-saver. The interface features four knobs and four buttons that are assignable to any parameter of any device. Multiple parameters can be assigned to an individual knob or button, permitting incredibly complex sound shaping capabilities with just a simple turn of a knob or press of a button.

In the next chapter, you will explore the power of the Combinator and learn how navigate and program its interface.

Chapter 7

THE
COMBINATOR

The Combinator

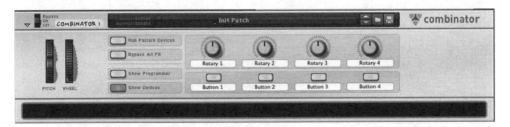

The Combinator is by far the most complex and creatively useful device offered by Reason. This device allows for the saving and recalling of any number of devices, including instruments, effects, mixers, and pattern generators. Once saved the patch (or combi) can be recalled, no matter how complex the setup is.

Imagine spending hours crafting a sound, which includes a mixer, several layered synthesizers, and multiple effects. And now imagine having to create the same patch all over again in a different song. The Combinator is a huge time-saver.

Beyond sound creation, there are a number of dedicated multi-effects combis including the Mastering Combi, with all the M-Class Mastering effects. Each mastering combi offers a different type of preset setup. The Combinator nests all the devices within the box at the bottom of the interface. By selecting Show Programmer, you can route any button or knob of any instrument or effect to the four knobs/buttons on the Combinator. Several parameters can then be controlled from a single knob or button.

When asked, "What's my favorite instrument in Reason?" my answer is consistently, "The Combinator." Let's explore some of the presets of the Combinator and get a feel for how to build a simple instrument.

Exploring Combinator Presets

Select Combinator from the Create menu.

From the patch browser, navigate to Combinator Patches > Performance Patches > Arpeggiated folder and select the As Falls Victoria Falls patch.

Layers

Play a few notes. You'll hear a complex, layered patch with multiple synthesizers, arpeggiators, and effects. Feel free to adjust some of the knobs and buttons to hear how the sound is changed. Most notable changes can be heard by engaging the Arp Mute and Pad Mute buttons and changing the Pad Timbre and Arp Speed knobs.

I chose this patch to demonstrate how complex a Combinator can be.

Let's look under the hood to see how it was created.

Show Devices

If it's not already displayed, hit the Show Devices button, located on the bottom left of the Combinator interface.

Next, hold down the Option/Alt key on your computer keyboard, while clicking the Unfold triangle of any device within the Combinator's device window.

This is a quick way to unfold all the devices at once, as opposed to the tedious task of unfolding each instrument individually. Incidentally, you can do the same from the rack to fold and unfold all of the devices; a real time- and space saver.

Within the Combinator are three synthesizers, two arpeggiators, and multiple effects, which are all routed through a mixer and compressor before connecting to the Combinator's output. Tab around to the back of the rack and view the complex routing.

Next, tab to the front view of the Combinator and press the Show Programmer button on the Combinator interface (just above the Show Devices button).

Show Programmer

There are two sections of the programmer: Key Mapping and Modulation Routing.

Key Mapping

Key Mapping contains a list of the twenty devices within the Combinator.

Grab the vertical navigation bar located on the right side of the Key Mapping section and drag down to view all the devices.

Next, select Joy Pad (Device 10) from the device list on the left. Once selected, the horizontal bar on the Joy Pad pane becomes highlighted and all the parameters at the bottom of the Key Mapping section become active.

Note Data

This group of parameters controls how the incoming note data are recognized and processed.

Receive Notes

This sets whether the current instrument will recognize incoming note data.

Key Range Lo

This sets the lowest key on your controller keyboard in which this device will play.

Key Range Hi

This sets the highest key on your controller keyboard in which this device will play.

Velocity Range Lo

This sets the lowest range of velocity in which the triggered note will play.

Velocity Range Hi

This sets the highest range of velocity in which the triggered note will play.

Transpose

This offers a transposition offset of the device.

Performance Controllers

Performance Controllers allow sound to be manipulated in real time.

Pitch Bend

By checking this, the device responds to Pitch Bend data.

Modulation Wheel

By checking this, the device responds to Modulation wheel data.

Breath

By checking this, the device will respond to Breath controller data.

Expression

By checking this, the device will respond to Expression controller data.

Sustain

By checking this, the device will respond to Sustain Pedal controller data.

After Touch

By checking this, the device will respond to After Touch messages. Only keyboard controllers with After Touch will generate this type of message.

Modulation Routing

The Modulation Routing window is located on the right side of the Show Programmer window. This is where you can assign any number of parameters to be controlled by a number of sources, including the four onboard knobs and buttons found on the Combinator interface.

With the Joy Pad device still selected, you can see in the Modulation Routing window that Knobs 1 and 2 are routed to the Pad Timbre and Drive knob on the Thor synthesizer. If you were view the Thor while moving the Pad Timbre and Drive knob on the Combinator interface, you'd see the Thor knobs being adjusted.

There are ten slots in the Modulation Routing section of the programmer.

Source

The Source column has any number of controller types. Pressing on the downward triangle of each slot reveals an extensive list of possible controls.

Target

The Target column has any number of destinations where the Source control is routed. Pressing the downward triangle reveals an extensive slot of destinations.

Minimum and Maximum

To the right of the Target column are the Minimum and Maximum slots, which are used to set a range of scaleable values.

Splits

Another popular function of Combinators is their ability to program a split. Where a layer has two or more instruments playing simultaneously, a split divides the keyboard controller into two or more parts, each playing a single instrument.

Let's have a look at a split preset.

Navigate to Combinator Patches > Performance Patches > Splits and select the patch Ac Bass & Vibraphone Split.

This is patch contains a line mixer, two NNXT samplers, an EQ, and an RV7000 reverb unit.

By opening the programmer, you will see that the Bass Instrument Key range has been set from C–2 to C3 on the key mapping, while the Vibraphone is mapped from C-sharp 3 to G8.

If you play notes below C3, you hear bass sounds, whereas notes above C-sharp 3 will trigger the sounds of the Vibraphone.

The modulation routing is set to control the room settings of the RV7000 reverb unit.

Song Starters

Another really fun type of preset are the Song Starters, also found the Performance patches.

Navigate to Combinator Patches > Performance Patches > Song Starters and select Ecstatic Salvation.

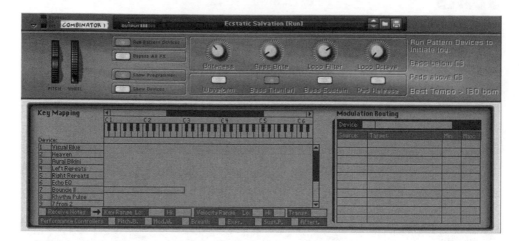

This Combinator even has directions on how to play the instrument written on the right side of the interface. Press Run and have fun!

As you can see, Combinators are incredibly powerful. They allow you to tap into the ability to play multiple instruments at once and give you dedicated control over sound-shaping controls and parameters.

Chapter 8
PATTERN SEQUENCING

The Concept

Before the advent of the digital synthesizer and MIDI, all controls for synthesizers and sequencers were in the form of analog control voltages (CV). Even though Reason is completely digital, Propellerhead has adopted the architecture and nomenclature of this bygone era, which provides a simplicity to physically routing cables between a device's CV inputs and its outputs.

In this chapter, you'll explore how to set up and program the Matrix Analog Pattern Sequencer and the RPG-8 Monophonic Arpeggiator.

The Matrix Pattern Sequencer

Let's begin by creating a 14:2 mixer and a Subtractor synthesizer.

On the Subtractor, click the Browse Patch button and select the Fat VeloBass patch from the Bass folder.

Select the Subtractor synthesizer, then from the Create drop-down menu click Matrix Pattern Sequencer.

The Matrix Pattern Sequencer is loaded into the rack just under the Subtractor. Now, tab around to the rear of the rack and take a closer look at the cabling.

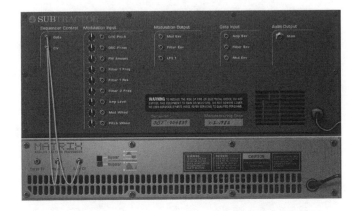

Besides the normal audio routing that connects the Subtractor to the mixer, you will find two more cables running from the Note CV and Gate output of the Matrix to CV and Gate inputs of the sequencer control of the Subtractor. The Note CV contains the pitch information, while the Gate controls the duration of the note.

Now, tab back to the front of the rack. You will next explore the matrix interface.

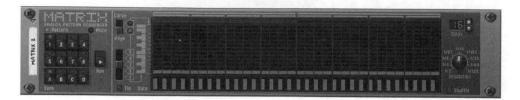

The matrix is broken into two sections, the Pattern Control section and the Sequencer Control section.

The Pattern Section

The Pattern section is divided into four banks (A–D) with eight patterns per bank, giving you a total of thirty-two patterns per device. You can switch between the banks and patterns simply by selecting their respective controls. It is possible to record an automated pattern selection onto a pattern lane. It is also possible to utilize the feature Copy Pattern to Track, which will print the currently selected pattern onto a track between the L and R locators. You'll explore the different ways to record and arrange with patterns in the next section, but first, let's look at how to program in the Sequencer Control section.

Types of CV Data

The matrix sequencer is capable of generating three types of data; Note CV, Gate CV, and Curve CV.

Note and Gate CV

This is the default setup when working with the matrix and is a great means of generating synth lines.

The main part of the sequencer is designed in a matrix format with individual horizontal blocks representing notes. A one-octave piano keyboard is located on the left side of the sequencer, with a five-way switch to change octaves (1 being the lowest octave). By default, the Octave switch is set to 3.

The vertical blocks at the bottom of the sequencer window control the Gate information for each note. Velocity for each note is controlled by the height of each vertical Gate block.

Curve CV

Curve CV is used to control parameters other than Note and Gate CV. Clicking the switch above the Octave selection switch activates this. Switching from Keys to Curve changes the setting to a secondary sequencer that allows for the sequencing of CV Curve data.

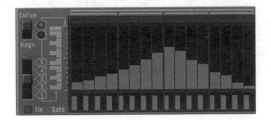

Here you'll see a simple up–down curve programmed into the sequencer. Notice how the sequencer window has changed from Note CV blocks to vertical lines, which allow for smoother, more precise control over the desired parameter. Note that even though the Gate sequencer data is still visible, it has no bearing on the control of the Curve CV.

Matrix Sequencer Programming

Note CV and Gate Programming

Let's switch the Curve switch back to Keys, and program in a bass line.

The sequencer resolution and number of steps are set by the controls on the left side of the device. By default, the resolution is set to sixteenth notes, while the steps are set at 16, giving you a one-bar sequence. You'll use the defaults for your sequence.

Begin by moving down the octave switch from 3 to 2.

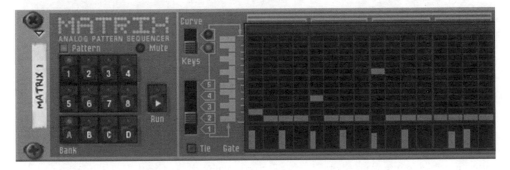

Now, program the sequencer so that it resembles the image above. To remove the Gate data, simply click and drag down until the vertical bar disappears. With no Gate information, the step now acts as a rest and no audio will be produced.

Hit the Run button, to listen to the sequence produced.

Now, let's create a variation on the sequence by pressing Command + C to copy. Select Pattern 2 and press Command + V to paste the data.

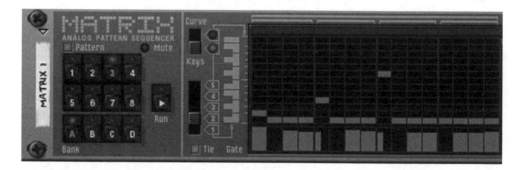

Fill in any unused Gate slots with a low-velocity Gate bar. Pattern 2 should be set to look like the image above.

Select Pattern 3 and press Command + V. This should paste the copied Pattern 1 into Pattern slot 3.

Just below the Octave switch control, you will see a button labeled Tie Gate. When enabled, any Gate data selected will appear to have a "fatter" bar and will create the effect of a longer note. You're using a sixteenth-note resolution, so if you tie two notes together at the same pitch, they are effectively played as eighth notes.

If you tie two gates together at different note pitches, it creates a portamento effect, where the first note slides into the second note. This effect was made popular in the "acid" style of bass line often produced by a TB303.

With the Tie Gate button enabled, now re-create the sequence pattern shown above.

Curve CV Programming

Copy Pattern 2 to Pattern 4 by using the same Command +C and Command + V method.

By default, the Curve CV output is not cabled to anything, so to program the effect, you must first decide what parameter you wish to control with the Curve CV. This is done with the Modulation wheel.

Tab to the rear of the rack and now cable the Curve CV output to the Mod Wheel input. Move the dial to the left of the Mod Wheel input all the way to the right, to maximize the effect.

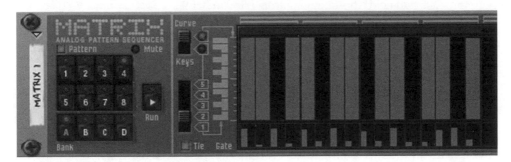

Tab back to the front of the rack and change the Keys switch to Curve. Next, re-create the sequence pattern shown above.

Recording Patterns to the Sequencer Window

There are two ways to work with patterns created with the Matrix Pattern Sequencer. The first is by recording the pattern in real time and the second is by using the Pencil tool to draw in the desired pattern information.

Recording in Real Time

To record pattern information, you first need to create a pattern lane for the data.

The easiest way is to right-click on the Pattern section of the matrix and select Edit Automation.

The same results can be obtained by selecting the matrix track in the sequencer window and selecting Create Pattern / Loop Lane from the Edit menu.

Once the pattern lane has been created, set the SPL to Bar 1, located on the sequencer page.

With Pattern 1 selected, click the Record button on the transport. As the SPL approaches Bar 3, select Pattern 2. Stop recording when the SPL reaches Bar 7.

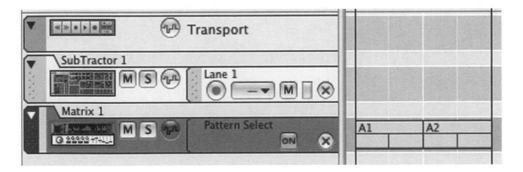

You should see Patterns A1 and A2 recorded onto the matrix track on the sequencer page.

Drawing Patterns

From the Tool Palette tools, select the Pencil tool. With the Pencil tool, click and hold while dragging from Bar 5 to Bar 7.

Again, click and hold while dragging from Bar 7 to Bar 9.

You'll notice that the new patterns are set to Pattern A1.

Select the Arrow from the Tools palette and then select the third pattern. A downward-facing arrow should now be displayed in the middle of the pattern. Click and hold on this and then select Pattern / Loop 3.

Do the same for the fourth pattern and select Pattern / Loop 4.

Convert Pattern Automation to Notes

Another way to work with the patterns generated by the matrix is to convert the patterns into a MIDI clip.

With the matrix track selected on the sequencer page, select Convert Pattern Automation to Notes from the Edit menu.

You'll notice that the Pattern button on the matrix has been turned off and the notes of the patterns have been replaced as MIDI clips on a newly created lane. If you were to hit play, you wouldn't hear anything, as the matrix doesn't produce any sounds. It can only generate patterns. So you now have to move the new MIDI clip on to the Subtractor track.

One drawback to this feature is the Curve CV data are not converted; only Note CV and Gate data are converted.

The RPG-8 Monophonic Arpeggiator

The RPG-8 is a pattern generator, but unlike the Matrix Pattern Sequencer, it requires MIDI note data and does not have the ability to store preset patterns. It is what I call a "live" performance tool and is capable of creating complex rhythms and patterns "on the fly."

The RPG-8 doesn't generate sounds on its own; you'll need to first create an instrument and then cable it to the RPG-8.

Let's begin by creating a Subtractor. From the Patch Browser, select Acid Saw 2 from the Monosynths folder.

This will show up on Channel 2 of your 14:2 mixer.

Let's also mute the first track on your mixer, which has the Matrix/Subtractor combo, so that you are only listening to the RPG8/Subtractor.

Next, with the newly created Subtractor selected, select RPG-8 Monophonic Arpeggiator from the Create menu.

Tab to the rear of the rack and confirm how the cabling works.

As with the matrix, you'll find the Note CV Out and the Gate CV Out of the RPG-8 are connected to the Note and Gate input of the sequencer control of the Subtractor.

You will also find that the Mod Wheel CV Out and the Pitch Bend CV Out are connected to the Mod Wheel and Pitch Bend input of the Modulation Input section of the Subtractor. This allows for the Modulation wheel and Pitch Bend data to be passed through the RPG-8 from your MIDI keyboard controller to the Subtractor.

The RBG-8 Interface

The RPG-8 is divided into three sections: MIDI-to-CV Converter, Arpeggiator, and Pattern.

MIDI-to-CV Converter

The MIDI-to-CV Converter section is displayed on the left side of the interface. It takes incoming MIDI messages and converts them to CV and Gate messages.

Velocity

The Velocity dial allows for control over how the RPG-8 interprets incoming velocity information. By default, the Velocity dial is set to Manual, which passes the incoming data through to the synthesizer, thereby allowing for flexibility, as you now have the ability to change the velocity response depending how hard (or quickly) you strike a key.

By changing from Manual to Fixed, you can set a constant velocity value independent of how you play your keyboard controller. The setting can range from 0, which outputs no sound, to 127, the loudest possible velocity setting.

Hold

The Hold button will latch on to any MIDI notes played and continues to run. You can change the sequence by pressing a new MIDI note or chord (several notes played simultaneously).

Octave Shift

The Octave Shift section shifts the incoming MIDI data up or down over three octaves, regardless of which octave was used to generate the original data.

Arpeggiator

The Arpeggiator section is located in the middle section and controls the generated patterns.

Mode

The Mode section controls the direction of the pattern based on notes played.

By focusing your attention on the Pattern section, you can see a visual representation of the patterns being generated. Try hitting three notes at once and switching between the different modes.

Up

Generates an upward pattern, playing the lowest note first and continuing up the scale.

Down

Generates a downward pattern, starting from the highest note and continuing down the scale.

Up + Down

Generates a pattern that starts with the lowest note played and continues up to the highest note, and then plays back down to the first note.

Random

Randomly selects the order of the notes played.

Manual

Notes are played in the order in which they are input.

Octave

The Octave section sets the range of how many octaves the pattern will scale.

Octave 1

Selecting this will cause the notes to play within the same octave played.

Octave 2

Selecting this will cause the notes played to play in the same octave and then repeat one octave above. Random further causes the generated pattern to alternate randomly between two octaves.

Octave 3

Selecting this will have the same effect as Octave 2, but increases the range to three octaves.

Octave 4
Selecting this will have the same effect as Octave 2 or 3, but increases the range to four octaves.

Insert
This section creates variations by repeating certain notes in a predetermined order.

Off
No change.

Low
The lowest note is repeated between every second note.

High
The highest note is repeated between every second note.

3–1
The generated pattern plays three notes forward and steps one note back, and then repeats.

4–2
The generated pattern plays four notes forward and steps two notes back, and then repeats.

Rate
Controls the speed of the Arpeggiator.

Sync
When activated, the Arpeggiator speed is locked to the song tempo as determined by note value (e.g., an eighth or a sixteenth).

Free
When this is selected, the Arpeggiator runs freely within a range of 0.1 Hz to 250 Hz.

Gate Length
This determines the length of each note. The default duration is dependent on the Rate selected. Moving the dials to the left shortens the duration, whereas moving them to the right increases it. A setting of 0 has no output, whereas a setting of 127 ties the durations together.

Single Note Repeat
Determines how the Arpeggiator responds to single notes. When this is active, a single note is repeated. When unselected, single notes will not trigger the Arpeggiator, only two notes or more will create a response.

Pattern
The Pattern section is located to the right of the interface and provides visual feedback of the pattern generated by the Arpeggiator.

Pattern Editor
By engaging the Pattern Editor button, you can gain more control over the generated pattern, with the ability to create rests within the Arpeggiator.

Steps + or –

This setting allows you to change the number of steps within the pattern. By default, the pattern is set to its maximum of sixteen steps. Pressing the + or – button will increase or decrease the number of steps respectively.

Shuffle

The Shuffle button engages a global swing. This can add a nice rhythmic effect to the patterns generated.

Using the RPG-8

Putting the RPG-8 to use is quite simple. Cable it to an instrument, adjust some of the parameters, and then play your MIDI controller.

Let's take a look at some ideas for generating patterns.

My favorite modes to generate patterns are the Random and Manual modes. I'm also a huge fan of the Insert section with the 3–1 and 4–2 settings.

In this patch, I set up the RPG-8 to generate a bass line. Using two octaves limits the range so that it stays in the low frequency area. The Random setting ensures that the bass line mutates every bar.

Within the Pattern section, I used the Random pattern feature found in the Edit drop-down menu.

To use this, first make sure to have the RPG-8's Pattern editor turned on. In the Edit menu, you'll find other several options that can be used to affect the pattern.

Edit Menu Options for Pattern Editor

For the Edit functions to have an effect, there must be a pattern in the Pattern editor. Some functions will not have an effect if all the steps are either active or deactivated.

Shift Pattern Left or Right

As the functions suggests, this will shift the current pattern either one step to the left or right, respectively.

Randomize Pattern

This will randomize the current pattern in the Pattern editor. Selecting this function repeatedly will result in different outcomes every time it is used.

Alter Pattern

This will alter the current pattern and is a great way to quickly change patterns. It is not as extreme of an effect as using the Random function.

Invert Pattern

Turns all notes to rests and all rests to notes.

Arpeggiator Notes to Track

This is one of my favorite features, because I prefer to work with MIDI clips when arranging. For this to work, first you'll need to record a MIDI clip to the RPG-8 track.

I recorded a two-bar loop of a C-minor chord (C2, D-sharp 2, G2).

Next, select the target track on the sequencer page. This is where you wish the arpeggiated sequence to be directed.

This is usually the instrument cabled to the RPG-8. In this case, it would be the Subtractor with the Acid 2 patch.

Now, select the RPG-8 from the rack and click Arpeggio Notes to Track from the Edit drop-down menu.

A new MIDI clip will be created from the output of the RPG-8 onto the Subtractor track. Be sure to mute the RPG-8 track from the sequencer track list, to avoid double triggers.

Conclusion

As you can see, the Matrix Pattern Sequencer and RPG-8 Monophonic Arpeggiator are incredibly powerful tools to have available in your programming arsenal. Spending some time experimenting with these devices can inspire you to create new and different types of patterns quickly and efficiently.

Chapter 9

CREATING AN ARRANGEMENT

Before You Begin

When starting to write a song, I personally find that it is important to be in the right mind set. I always recommend being well rested and having eaten some food to ensure solid focus. It's also important to take a ten-minute break every forty-five minutes to an hour to help maintain adequate performance. I also find that it's easier to block out at least three hours to work uninterrupted. There's nothing more frustrating than having the phone ring every five minutes, so you may wish to minimize such distractions. I'm also not a fan of working more than eight hours in one session, but if you're in the "zone," then by all means, run with it. However you choose to work, be sure to keep yourself hydrated and, again, take regular breaks.

The Setup

In Chapter 3–Getting Started, under Preferences, you selected the song start Empty Rack. In this chapter, let's change your song start preference to Built In. This will automatically create a Mixer 14:2 and a Mastering Combinator, perfect for starting a song. After you've set the preference to Built In, select New from the File menu

Now, let's dive in to creating an arrangement and get something produced. On the Transport window at the bottom of the rack, first set the tempo to 140.000 bpm, then enable the Loop button, and finally, deselect the Blocks button.

Setting the Mastering Suite

Before you begin, you need to bypass the M-Class EQ in the Mastering Suite Combi. Click the triangle in the upper left corner of the device, which will unfold the Combinator interface. Next, click the Show Devices button to reveal Mastering Effects. Bypass the M-Class EQ by selecting the Bypass switch, located in the upper left corner of the EQ. The only active device in the Mastering Combi should be the M-Class Maximizer. Having the Maximizer on will prevent any digital clipping, which safeguards both your hearing and your studio monitors.

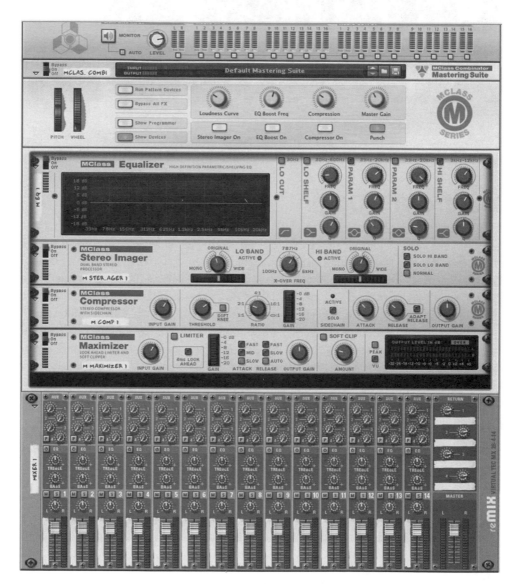

Creating a Drum Track

Now you are ready to select the mixer. From the Create drop-down menu, select ReDrum Drum Computer. It's important to let Reason know what device you'd like the ReDrum to be connected to. You'll see a blue highlight border the mixer, letting you know that the device has been selected.

Once the ReDrum is created, you'll see the Channel 1 label on the mixer has the text ReDrum 1 written next to it. This lets you know that the proper cabling has occurred. You are now ready to set a patch.

On the ReDrum, select the Browse Patch button, and navigate to the DrumNbass folder to then select the patch labeled DrumNbass Kit 01.

By default, the first channel of the ReDrum is selected. At the top of Channel 1, you'll see three buttons: M (Mute), S (Solo), and a triangle (Play button). Click on the Play button or triangle and you will hear the sound of a Kick Drum.

It is possible to play and record the ReDrum with your MIDI controller keyboard, effectively using ReDrum as a drum module. Octave C1 will play Channel 1, while C-sharp 1 will play Channel 2, and so on. Instead, however, you are going to be using ReDrum as a drum machine by activating and utilizing the Pattern section.

First, change the number of steps on the ReDrum from 16 to 32, by clicking on the upward-facing triangle next to the Steps section, which appears as a red numerical display located at the bottom center of the device. Click the Run button. The red LED will start moving through Steps 1 through 16. ReDrum will only display sixteen steps at a time, so once the LED has reached 17, it will disappear from view as it cycles through Steps 17 through 32. To see Steps 17 through 32, click and hold the Edit Steps Select switch and move it up to the 17–32 option. The LED will now be running through Steps 17 through 32, and will then disappear as it goes back to Steps 1 through 16.

Move the Edit Steps Select switch back to 1–16 and then select Steps 1 and 7. The Kick Drum on Channel 1 will play Steps 1 and 7 as the red LED cycles through the pattern.

Now, click the Select button on Channel 2. Then click on Step 9 on the sequencer. You will hear the sound of a Snare.

Move the Edit Step Select button up to 17–32 and select 9. Click the Select button on Channel 1 and click on Steps 1, 4, 7, and 15.

You have now created a two-bar pattern using Channels 1 and 2 on the ReDrum.

Copy Pattern to Track

Copy Pattern to Track is a feature similar to the Copy Loop to Track on the Dr. OctoRex Loop Player. It will copy the current pattern on to the sequencer page between the Left and Right locators. (By default, the Left locator is set to 1.1.1.0 and the Right locator is set to 9.1.1.0.) With the ReDrum track selected in the sequencer window, select the Edit drop-down menu. Select the Copy Pattern to Track command, located near the bottom of the Edit menu. On the ReDrum Track on the sequencer, a MIDI clip is now created spanning eight bars.

When you press Play on the Transport window; you'll hear what is called double triggering. Essentially what is occurring is the same MIDI information is being transmitted twice, simultaneously: The MIDI data on the sequencer are being sent to the ReDrum and the ReDrum sequencer is also playing the same notes. The resulting sound is known as phasing and is undesirable. This can be easily remedied by deselecting the Enable Pattern

Section button on the ReDrum, located above the Run button. Now the ReDrum is being controlled solely by the MIDI data on the sequencer page.

Let's do a bit more programming with the ReDrum's onboard pattern sequencer. Reenable the Enable Pattern Section button and select Pattern 2 from the pattern selector.

Next, select Channel 9 on the ReDrum and click every odd-numbered step: 1, 3, 5, 7, 9, 11, 13, and 15.

Now press, Run on the ReDrum. You are hearing an eighth-note High Hat pattern. To give the pattern a little variation, let's change the velocity of every other step. First, select Soft under the dynamic section of the ReDrum and then reselect Steps 3, 7, 11, and 15. This will afford a less mechanical feeling to the High Hat pattern by softening the velocity for selected steps.

From the Edit menu, select Copy Pattern to Track. A new lane will appear, along with an additional MIDI clip containing the High Hat pattern you just created. Deselect the Enable Pattern Section button and hit Play on the Transport window.

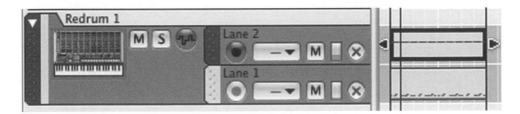

Congratulations! You've just programmed your first beat with the ReDrum Drum Computer. With this fundamental in place, you are ready to proceed.

Now, let's record a bass line using the Subtractor.

Recording Bass Line A

From the Create menu, select the Subtractor. You'll notice that the Subtractor will automatically cable it's self to the mixer on Channel 2.

Next, click the Browse Patch button and select ResonBass from the Bass folder.

On the Transport window, click the Q-Rec button to activate the Quantize While Recording function. This will automatically quantize your playing in real time, which proves to be a real time-saver.

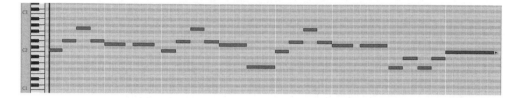

Set your R locator to 5 to create a four-bar loop. Now record the bass line displayed above. The notes are in the C2 octave unless otherwise noted. The notes are C, D-sharp, G, D-sharp, D, D, C, D-sharp, G, D-sharp, D, G1, C, D-sharp, G, D-sharp, D, D, G1, A-sharp 1, G1, A-sharp 1, and C. When you have finished recording, make sure the note events are the correct length. Selecting each note and adjusting the right side so that it snaps to the nearest sixteenth value easily accomplish this.

If you don't consider yourself a great keyboard player, another way to create this sequence is to draw the notes into a blank MIDI clip. To create a blank MIDI clip, select the Pencil tool from the Tool Palette tools and draw in a MIDI clip from Bar 1 to Bar 5. Click the Edit Mode button in the upper left corner of the sequencer page. This will bring you into the blank MIDI clip. Make sure the Pencil tool is engaged and simply draw in the notes to match the bass line above.

Once you've completed the bass line and confirmed that the durations of each note event are accurate, click the Edit Mode button again to view the sequence from the Arrangement view. Copy the MIDI clip by using keyboard command Control + C and then paste it using keyboard command Control + V.

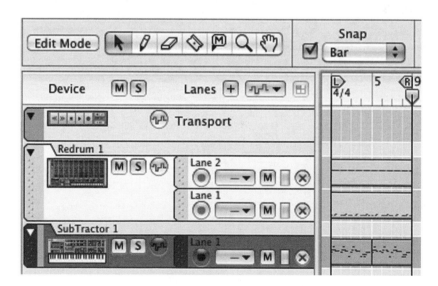

Your sequence page should look like this.

Next, let's make another MIDI clip with a variation on your bass line.

Recording Bass Line B

Move your R locator to Bar 13 and your L locator to Bar 9.

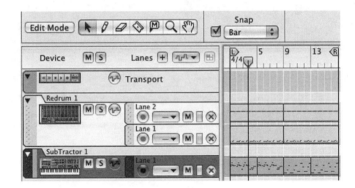

Record or pencil in the following notes in the C2 octave: C, D-sharp, G, C, D-sharp, G, D, A, F-sharp, D, F-sharp, G.

Make a copy of the MIDI sequence with the Control + C and Control + V method.

Next, copy your MIDI clips from your ReDrum track. Select both the High Hat and Kick/ Snare clips and Control and Control.

Now, set the locators around the entire sixteen-bar sequence. The fastest and easiest way to do this is by rubber-band selecting all the clips and pressing the letter P on your keyboard.

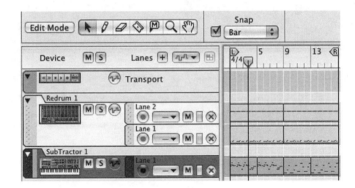

You now have the foundation with which to start building your arrangement. Next, you are going to create some additional instruments.

Creating Layers

Create a Malstrom synthesizer by selecting Create > Malstrom, located in the Create drop-down menu. Notice that the Malstrom is automatically connected to Channel 3 on your mixer.

Click on the Browse Patch button and select Gangsta Lead from the Monosynths folder.

Next rubber-band select all the MIDI clips shown on the Subtractor track in the sequencer window. With all four clips selected, click and hold with your mouse while simultaneously holding down the Option/Alt key on your computer keyboard. With Option/Alt and the mouse held down, drag a copy of the Subtractor MIDI clips into the Malstrom track. Remember to release the Option/Alt key last, otherwise you'll end up moving the MIDI clips and not copying them. This method of copying is referred to as the Option/Alt + Drag method.

Hit the Play button on the Transport window to hear your sequence. You should hear the doubling of the bass line with the Subtractor playing the Bass Line and the Malstrom playing the Gangsta Lead patch. This technique is referred to as layering. Having the same MIDI information playing two different synthesizers is the fastest and easiest way to create new and inspiring sounds. The sum of multiple tracks within the layer is infinitely more interesting than the individual parts on their own.

Next, let's create a layer for the ReDrum track.

On the Create menu, select ReDrum. Click the Browse Patch button and select House Kit 07 from the House Kits folder. On the upper left corner of the ReDrum is the Master Level. Raise the value of this level from 100 to 110.

Next, rubber-band select the Kick/Snare MIDI clip, Option/Alt + Drag the clip to the ReDrum 2 track on the sequencer page, and then press Play.

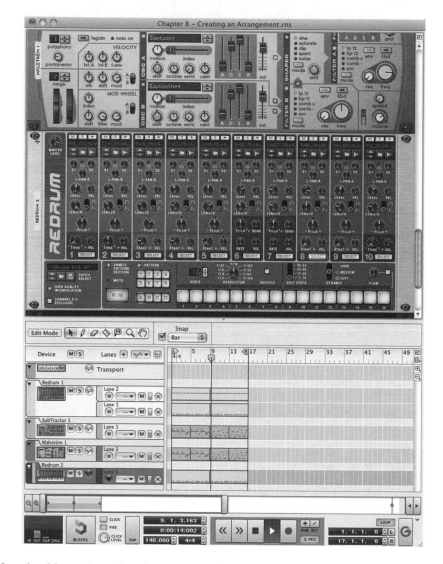

You should now have four instruments playing simultaneously. ReDrum 1 is playing the Kick/Snare and High Hat pattern, while ReDrum 2 has layered the Kick/Snare pattern, creating a layer for the Kick and Snare. The Subtractor and Malstrom are layered with both playing the Bass Line patterns.

Using the Tool Window

Now, you are going to add a Thor and an additional Malstrom, but this time by a different method, using the Device Panel in the Tools window (F8). To create a Thor, simply double-click on the Thor icon. Repeat the same process to add another Malstrom.

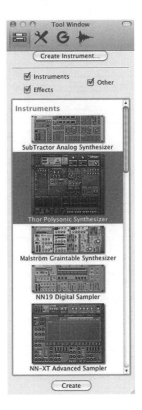

Next, click the Browse Patch button on the Thor and select Fifth Triggers, found in the Rhythmic folder. While on the Malstrom, click the Browse Patch button and select JapanPluck, located in the Polysynths folder.

Now, copy the MIDI clips from the Subtractor track to both the Thor and Malstrom 2 tracks.

Next, transpose the Thor MIDI clips up one octave by using the Transpose Notes function of the Sequencer Tools window. Change the number of semitones to 12 and then press Apply.

Organization

Now that you've got six instruments going, you might find things can get a little confusing. As such, it's always a great idea to relabel your tracks. By double-clicking on the instrument name on the tracks of your sequencer window, you can easily rename the label for each instrument with the name of the current patch. Note how each name change is reflected on the track, instrument, and mixer channel label.

Another useful technique for organization is to use separate colors for the different variations on your MIDI clips. Select the MIDI clips from Bar 1 to Bar 9 on the ResonBass, Gangsta Lead, Fifth Triggers, and JapanPluck tracks and with the clips selected, navigate to Color on the Edit menu and select Olive Green. You can see how this makes visual organization easier and creates order.

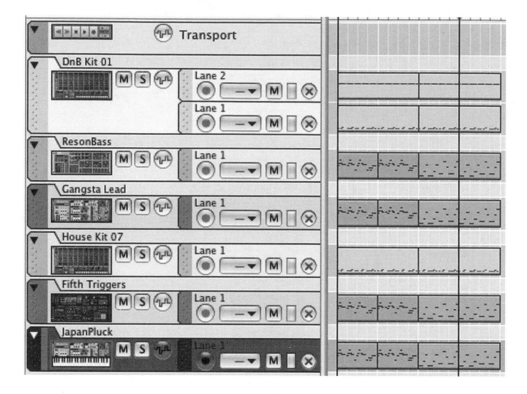

Arranging

Your next task is to start arranging your clips to form a song. Typically, a song will be broken into different sections: an intro, an A section A, a B section, a breakdown, and an outro. You've already done the hard part, which was writing the A and B sections. Your A section is now green, while the blue section is referred to as B.

Select all of the MIDI clips by either rubber-band selecting or using the keyboard command Control + A. Now copy the clips by using the Option/Alt + Drag method. Copy them a second time and you will have clips starting at Bar 1 and ending at Bar 49.

Intro

Now you'll work on the intro. The idea is to introduce elements of the song gradually, so by around measure 17 everything is playing.

First, remove some clips by selecting them and hitting Delete.

Then delete the Kick/Snare clip at Bar 1 on the DnB Kit 01 track.

Next, resize the High Hat clip so it begins at Bar 5. This is done by selecting the clip and grabbing the left triangle before moving it to Bar 5.

With the exception of the JapanPluck track, select all the clips from Bar 1 to Bar 17 and hit Delete.

On the JapanPluck track, select the A (Green) section and delete. Next, copy the B (blue) clips to fill in the gap at Bar 1.

Another useful method of arranging is by muting clips instead of deleting them. It will give you same effect as deleting clips, but also has the flexibility of allowing you to return to or easily retrieve a previous idea by unmuting the clips instead of replaying or recopying clips.

To mute, first select the A (green) section clips on the Fifth Triggers track and hit the M key on your computer keyboard. Next, select the B (blue) section clips on the JapanPluck track and hit the M key on your computer keyboard. The muted clips will now be displayed with diagonal bars across them.

Select the entire arrangement and copy to start at Measure 49, using Control + C.

Breakdown

Next you are going to focus on the breakdown sections of the song you are producing.

For your breakdown, you're going to use a total of four Combinators. So, your first step is to go ahead and create all four.

For Combinator 1, click the Patch Browser and select Hyperspace Explosion from the Synth FX folder.

For Combinator 2, click the Patch Browser and select Granular Sweep from the Textures and Musical FX folder.

For Combinator 3, click the Patch Browser and select The Underworld from the Textures and Musical FX folder.

For Combinator 4, click the Patch Browser and select Cymbal FX Pan from the Textures and Musical FX folder.

Don't forget to rename the tracks with the Patch name for the four Combinators you've just created.

Starting at Bar 49, record C3 for a duration of eight bars for the Hyperspace Explosion Track.

Next, record sixteen bars of C3 for the Granular Sweep track. Start this at Bar 49. At Bar 53, record twelve bars of C2 for the The Underworld track.

And finally, you will need to record the following:

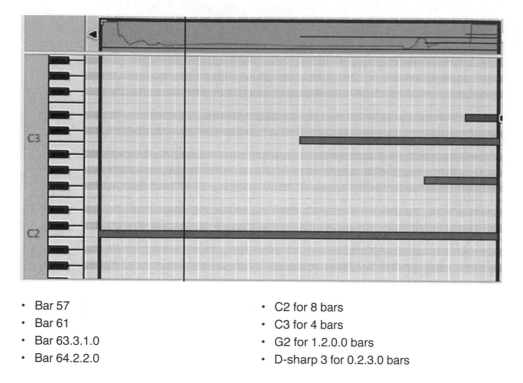

- Bar 57
- Bar 61
- Bar 63.3.1.0
- Bar 64.2.2.0

- C2 for 8 bars
- C3 for 4 bars
- G2 for 1.2.0.0 bars
- D-sharp 3 for 0.2.3.0 bars

You are, of course, free to record this in real time, but it may prove easier to use the Pencil tool method instead and then simply fine-tune the adjustments using the Inspector.

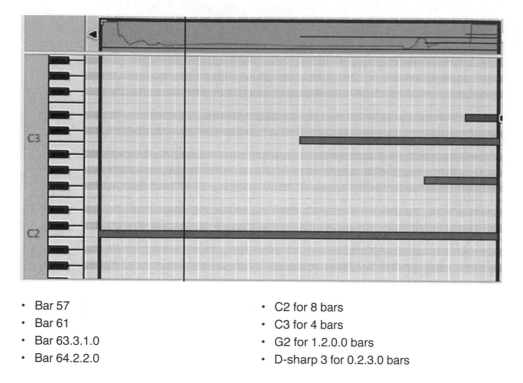

After listening to the breakdown a few times, push back the Granular Sweep, so that it begins at Bar 48.4.1.0. The sound fades up, so pushing back a quarter-note tightens up the timing. The easiest way to do this is to change the Snap value at the top of the sequencer window to 1/4 and grab the MIDI clip to move it back by 1/4.

Next, double-click on the Kick/Snare clip that starts at Bar 57.

Now, remove all the Kick Drums except for the ones that occur at:
- 60.4.1.0
- 61.1.1.0
- 62.4.1.0
- 63.1.1.0

Next, let's create a Kick Drum roll at the end of the Kick/Snare clip.

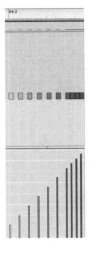

Use the Pencil tool to draw in eight Kick Drum notes, starting at Bar 64.3.1.0.
Change the Snap value to 1/32 and pencil in two more notes at:
- Bar 64.4.3.120
- Bar 64.4.4.120

Next, let's make the notes of the drum roll a crescendo, by creating a velocity ramp. With the Pencil tool selected, hold the Option key down. The Pencil tool will change into a cross. Click and hold at the velocity range of 16 and drag up diagonally to the upper right corner. Release the mouse first, then the Option key, and the velocity is now ramped so that it gets increasingly louder toward the end of the clip.

Adding Percussion

Next, you'll continue with the concept of introducing new elements as the song progresses, by adding percussion to the second half of your song.

First, create a Dr. OctoRex. Click on the Browse Patch button and then select the Percussion / Cajon 100-1 patch from the Percussion folder.

Move the L locator to Bar 65 and the R locator to Bar 73.

Unfold the Dr. OctoRex Programmer by clicking the triangle located at the bottom left of the instrument. With the first loop selected, click the Copy Loop to Track button.

Next, move the L locator to Bar 73 and the R locator to Bar 81.

Select the third loop on the Dr. OctoRex and click the Copy Loop to Track button.

To help identify the A and B sections of the Cajon track, let's change the color of the B clips you just created. On the sequencer page, rubber-band select the four clips between Bar 73 and Bar 81. With the clips selected, navigate to Color on the Edit menu and select Lilac. Finally, select the newly created clips on the Dr. OctoRex track and use Option/Alt + Drag to make a copy, placing them at Bar 81 to Bar 97.

Outro

Your next task is to create an outro for your song. Perform the following steps in order:

Copy three B (blue) clips of JapanPluck track to start at Bar 97.

Copy two B (blue) clips of ResonBass track to start at Bar 97.

Copy four B (Lilac) clips of Cajon track to start at Bar 97.

In essence, the outro is just a variation on the intro, with some additional percussion.

Ear Candy

And finally, to top things off, let's add a Reverse Crash Cymbal to your arrangement. This is a bit of "icing on the cake" and is often referred to as ear candy. I find it's useful to let the listener know that a change is about to happen and it also helps to soften the transitions.

Double-click on the High Hat track that begins at Bar 9 and navigate to the end of the clip. Change the Snap value from 1/16 to 1/32. With the Pencil tool, create a note for FX_ Photek at Bar 16.2.2.120.

Next, let's change the color of this clip. With the clip selected, navigate to Color on the Edit menu and select Slate Blue.

Change back to the Arrangement view and zoom out to see the entire arrangement. Now, copy the clip to Bars 41, 57, 89, and 97. Your track is done.

Chapter 10

THE ART AND SCIENCE OF MIXING

Before You Begin Mixing

When working in audio engineering, it is really necessary to use both sides of your brain. Using the clinical, analytical side enables you to focus on the science of sound, while the creative, artistic side allows you to work as if you are painting on an aural canvas. Although it can take many years of hard work and dedication to train ones ears properly, don't let that deter you. We all start from the same place and you'll be amazed at what you can accomplish with some steady effort and determination.

A few words of advice before you begin your mixing session work. It's really important to be well rested, but this especially holds true regarding your ears. Although you might feel inspired, the last thing you want to do is try to mix after you've come home from a noisy club or concert. You should always try to start a mixing session with fresh ears, and a good night's sleep does wonders. Also, as when composing, it's a good idea to have eaten a little something, to give you proper focus during the session. I also like to block out a solid four to eight hours of work time. Again, it is advisable to turn off the phone and close the Web browser, to minimize distractions. And remember to take a ten-minute break every forty-five minutes or so. You should take care to give your ears a rest and let your brain focus on something else, to maintain stamina. This will also prevent you from overtaxing your ears and to keep the mix fresh and in perspective.

I'm often asked, "What's the most important tool in your arsenal?" I never fail to respond strongly, "Your ears!" I cannot emphasize enough how important it is to protect your hearing. If you know you are going to a club or loud concert, be sure to bring along some hearing protection. Every pharmacy carries sets or packs of small disposable earplugs that you should have on hand. If you find you are not happy with the "muffled" sound these can result in, then I recommend making the investment in custom molded in-ear attenuators. You've only got one pair of ears and once you've damaged or lost your hearing, little can be done to get it back.

Another tool I use quite often is called the reference track. This is a commercially released, uncompressed track that I can use as a reference while I'm mixing. Don't presume that this is used to copy or re-create the mix anew. Rather, using a reference track allows my mind to recall what a proper mix sounds like, thereby helping me focus on how each instrument in the song should sound in relation to all the other instruments. It saves a lot of time and frustration to have a reference track available.

Mixing music can easily be compared to painting. We start off with a blank sonic canvas, and all the instruments used in our song serve as the subject components of our aural painting. Each sound can be equated to different shapes and colors. Just as painters use different styles of brushes to create textures on their canvas, our main "brush" is the mixing board itself. It allows us to blend the sounds together. Making a particular sound louder pushes the sonic image closer to us. The Pan knobs control the perception of where that sound exists on our canvas with regard to left, right, and center. As we move through this chapter, you'll learn about the mixing board and the basic tools it contains, so that you can use it effectively to shape your sound and bring your aural painting to vivid, stereo life.

Understanding the Mixer

The reMIX 14:2 mixer in Reason allows for the blending of up to fourteen mono or stereo tracks at a time. It gives you control over volume, panning, and basic EQ. This mixer also has four aux (auxiliary) tracks that will allow you to use effects to create a sense of space and depth.

Channel Strip

Let's start by looking at an individual channel on the mixer.

Each channel contains the following:
- Aux 1–4
- 2-Band Shelf EQ
- S—Solo
- M—Mute
- Pan pot—Left, Center, and Right
- Volume fader—Loudness Control
- Channel label—Name of instrument assigned or connected to track

All the channels on the mixer essentially do the same thing. It doesn't matter if the mixing board has 14 or 144 tracks. Every channel strip serves the same primary function. Learn to use one and you know them all. The only other section of the mixer you must become familiar with is the Master section. Fortunately, the 14:2 has a very simple Master section featuring a Master Fader that controls the overall loudness of your mix. It also contains dedicated aux returns.

Master Section

Aux returns interact with the aux sends on your channel strip. For every aux send, there's a dedicated aux return. (More on this later.)

The Master Fader is the level control for the Main Mix or Stereo Master Fader.

Gain Stage

One thing to always consider when mixing is the gain stage. There are several places in which to control the gain or loudness of your instruments. In addition to the faders on the mixer, all of the instruments in Reason have their own main volume control built into their respective control panels. The most important thing to keep in mind is to make sure you're not overdriving the Master Fader, also referred to as a Stereo Bus, on the mixer. Your goal is to leave enough headroom on each individual track to enable gain and adjustment by other means during the mixing process. If you make each track too loud, then you're actually making the task of mixing harder on yourself than it needs to be, because it's akin to painting yourself into a corner. Personally, I like to keep my mixing channels set more toward the middle, thereby leaving lots of room to boost the softer-sounding instruments. This will prevent overdriving of the Master Fader and further facilitate your mixing session.

Another thing to consider is that mixing is always subjective. There are no hard or fast rules when it comes to mixing; however, I'll be demonstrating some guidelines that you can follow. It's important to understand how these guidelines operate before attempting to deviate from them (like knowing the rules before you break them). As we move through this chapter, I'll be showing you insight into my approach to mixing. As you begin your journey into the realm of mixing, you'll start to develop your own style and approach to serve your sense of style and subjectivity.

The Static Mix

Let's begin your mixing session by setting up a static mix. A static mix is the starting point where you set your basic levels and pan control. It's called static because it's similar to a snapshot. In the next chapter, we'll explore automation to help make your mix more dynamic.

First, let's set up a loop around the most active section of your song. Looking at the sequencer window for this arrangement, I designate this to be located from Bar 65 to Bar 89. Next, rubber-band select around this section and hit P on your computer keyboard. The L and R locators will automatically wrap around the selected clips and the transport will begin to play.

Keep in mind, human hearing is quite sensitive and we can perceive the slightest adjustments to volume. In fact, an increase of just 3 dB is often perceived as twice as loud. A good guideline to follow when making volume adjustments is, "Less is more."

Drums

The first thing I like to do when setting up the static mix is to bring down all the faders to zero. I prefer to begin with ensuring my drum mix sounding its best.

Start this by bringing Channel 1 to 77. Next, bring Channel 4 to 72.

Channel 1, the DnB Kit, will provide the "character" for your Kick and Snare sounds. Channel 4, the House Kit, will add the oomph to your Kick and some additional crack to your Snare. You will use the House Kit to blend just underneath the DnB Kit without overpowering it.

Next, bring Channel 11, the Cajon, to 73. This may change a little later as you start to bring in additional sounds, but for now, this setting enables it to blend well with your main drum sound.

Bass

Bring Channel 2, the ResonBass track, to 59. Already, I can hear that the ResonBass will need a little equalization adjustment, as the low frequencies seem to be fighting a little with the Kick Drum sound. But you are focusing first on getting the static mix, so you'll return to this in a bit.

The idea here is to be able to clearly hear the drums and the bass sounds. Check this mix at different volumes and ensure that at low levels you should still be able to hear all of the parts clearly.

Bring Channel 5, or the Fifth Triggers, to 67; and Channel 6, the JapanPluck, to 63. These elements should blend well with the other elements, but certainly not be upfront or overpowering in the mix.

Synthesizers

Now, bring Channel 3, Gangsta Lead, to 61. This is your lead sound and plays throughout both the A and B sections of your arrangement, so this instrument should blend well but still be maintained as a focal point within the mix.

Now, move your attention to the breakdown section. Select the breakdown section and hit the letter P on the computer keyboard.

Channel 7, Hyperspace Explosion, is one of the first elements of your breakdown and thus it needs to be pretty loud to effectively compete with the rest of the arrangement as it is coming to a stop. It's a short blast of high-frequency sound, so if this element is too low, you'll lose its impact and the breakdown will seem weak. As such, let's bring this setting up to 77.

Channel 8, or the Granular Sweep, also begins playing at the top of the breakdown. It provides a lot of low-frequency content, builds over time, and lasts the duration of the entire breakdown. Bring this setting up to 55.

Channel 9, The Underworld, starts four bars into the breakdown and adds additional harmonic content as Hyperspace Explosion comes to an end. Likewise, bring this setting up to 55.

Channel 10, the Cymbal FX, adds some dissonance and tension to the breakdown. You're bringing it in at the end of the breakdown to add a little dramatic effect before the song kicks back in again. Bring this setting up to 52.

Understanding Sound

Now that the static mix is in order, let's focus on getting a better blend by using some additional effects. However, before you go too deeply into the effects, let's first talk a little about sound.

Sound moves in waves, and we use two primary measurements: frequency, measured in hertz (Hz) and amplitude, measured in decibels (dB).

In the following figure, you see the highest point of a waveform, referred to as a peak, is followed by a trough at the lowest point. The waveform moves through the peak and trough and starts again. This oscillation is referred to as a cycle. The number of cycles per second determines the frequency. A 30-Hz waveform has thirty cycles per second. Human beings can hear between the ranges of 20 and 20,000 Hz (20 kHz).

The amplitude of a waveform is measured as the distance from the centerline to the peak and/or trough. The larger the amplitude, the louder the sound becomes. To provide a point of reference, consider that a quiet room with minimal ambient noise registers at about 40 dB, whereas a rock concert or nightclub often regularly tops out at 130 dB or more.

Adding Effects

EQ

Equalizers are used to adjust the frequency and amplitude of your instruments so they blend correctly, resulting in a balanced sound.

Let's first set up the EQ on the ResonBass track. You could use the EQ on the reMIX 14:2 mixer, but it doesn't offer enough precise control. In my opinion, the basic EQ of the 14:2 is fine for controlling broader sounds, but lacks the precision of a parametric EQ. The PEQ-2 is a good contender, but I'm more inclined to go with the M-Class EQ, as it has four bands and always sounds fantastic.

Reason is smart enough to know how to automatically cable a device, provided you tell it which instrument you'd like to insert the effect to for mixing. In this case, you want to cable the M-Class EQ between the Subtractor and the mixer.

Start off by selecting the Subtractor. A blue border will appear around the Subtractor once it's selected. Next, select the M-Class EQ from the Create menu.

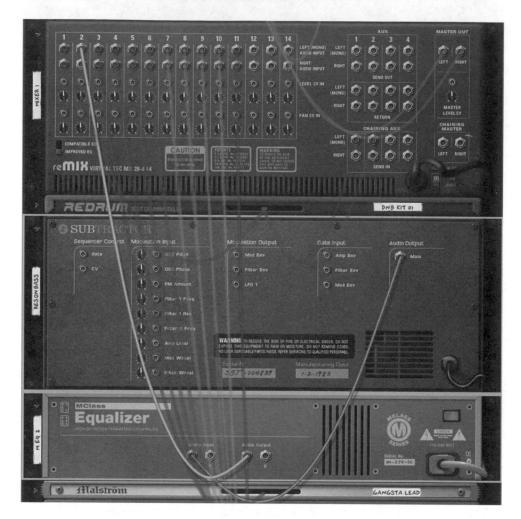

Press the Tab key on your computer keyboard and take a look at the rear of the rack. Instead of the Subtractor connecting directly to the mixer on Channel 2, you'll find the output of the Subtractor has been routed to the newly created M-Class EQ and the EQ routed to Channel 2 on the mixer. Press Tab again to toggle back to view the front of the rack.

Notice how Channel 2 on the mixer is now labeled M-EQ Left. The label on the mixer will change depending on the connection made. Let's change the name of the M-Class EQ to ResonBass EQ by double-clicking on the M-Class EQ label on the left side of the device and typing in the new name. The label on Channel 2 of the mixer will reflect these changes.

Now let's add an M-Class EQ on the Kick Drum of the ReDrum House Kit. If you were to select the ReDrum and create the EQ, the device would be automatically connected to the main out of the ReDrum. Normally this would be fine, but for this session you don't necessarily want the same EQ settings for the Clap sound as you would want for the Kick Drum. In this case, you need to first route the output of the Kick through an M-Class EQ, and then to an open channel on the mixer.

Let's begin by creating an M-Class EQ without utilizing Auto-routing. This is easily achieved by holding down the Shift key when creating the EQ.

First, select the ReDrum House Kit. Next, hold down the Shift key while selecting M-Class EQ from the Create menu. The EQ is created just underneath the ReDrum, but is not automatically cabled.

Now, press Tab to view the rear of the rack. Next, click and hold the Left output of Channel 1 of the ReDrum and quickly drag the cable to the left input of the EQ. By your selecting the left output of a stereo channel, the right output will automatically cable itself to the right input. This applies to all the stereo devices you will use.

Next, click and hold the Left output of the EQ and drag it up to the Left input of Channel 12 on the mixer. You now have the Kick Drum routed to channel 12 via an M-Class EQ. Hit Tab on the computer to view the front of the mixer and change the label on the EQ to Low Kick.

Your next step is to set a loop around Bar 65 to Bar 97. Solo Channel 12, or Low Kick, on the mixer and lower the volume fader to 72.

On the Low Kick EQ, turn on the Lo Cut button. This will filter out frequencies below 30 Hz. Next, turn on Param 1 and raise the Gain knob to +6.3 dB. Drag the Freq knob down to 52.4 Hz. While sweeping down the audio spectrum, you'll hear different frequencies being increased. Notice that between 52.4 and 47.7 Hz, the sound of the Kick is greatly enhanced. Next, grab the Q knob and move it leftward to 3.0.

Now that you've found the loudest frequency of your Kick, turn down Gain to –2.3 Hz. Notice how a lot of the boominess of the bass is removed. Again, don't forget that "less is more"! You don't want to remove too much bass, so this is an ideal balance.

Let's now solo the ResonBass on channel 2 of the mixer.

Enable the Lo Cut filter on the ResonBass EQ.

Next, enable Parm 1 and move the Freq knob to 52.7 Hz. Finally, turn down the Gain knob to –5.7 Hz and adjust the Q to 4.4.

Unsolo the ResonBass and Low Kick track and listen to the difference. Notice how, now, there's a nice balance between the Bass and Kick Drum, yet both are powerful and present.

You've already determined that the ResonBass and Low Kick are defining the low-end content for this track. Any other instruments that generate low frequencies are interfering with these instruments. The easiest way to determine if a sound is generating low frequencies is to solo the channel, turn on the EQ, and boost the Bass knob by turning to the right. If you hear a noticeable difference in the bass frequencies, then this channel should have its bass cut.

Start by engaging the EQ of Channel 5 on the mixer by clicking the On/Off button. Solo channel 5 and start increasing the bass by moving the Bass knob to the right. The Fifth Triggers patch seems to have bass percolating that is most noticeable on the transients, or initial attack, of the sound. Bring the Bass knob back to the center and unsolo the track. With the entire track playing, slowly decrease the bass by moving the Bass knob to the left. It's important to make adjustments to EQs while listening to the entire track. EQ-ing a soloed track is a waste of time because you lack proper reference as to how the EQ adjustments you are making will affect the entire mix.

Channel 6, the JapanPluck, has some low frequencies that can be cut, but if you cut too much of these, you will overly flatten the character of the instrument excessively. To avoid this, let's set the Bass knob at –20.

Channel 11, Cajon, has the same qualities, so setting the Bass knob at –22 will help with the overall mix.

Compression

A really useful tool that helps control amplitude is a compressor. This device makes louder sounds softer, and softer sound louder. It can help smooth out an erratic performance where the artist is playing too loudly or too softly. It can also be used to add punch to drums or change the overall perception of loudness of an entire mix. However, compression is one of the more difficult processors to use because it's hard to discern what is really happening to the signal (unlike an EQ, which is quite apparent). Keep in mind that the sounds you're working with are professionally produced samples. Just because EQ and compression are available for every sound, doesn't necessarily mean you need to use them on every track.

Reason has two compressors, the Comp-01 compressor and the M-Class compressor. Both work well for their intended purposes, but I find the M-Class compressor to have more control and produce a better overall sound.

Let's start by inserting an M-Class Compressor on your Clap track being generated by the ReDrum House Kit. If you recall, you've routed the Kick to a separate track on your mixer, so the only sound being generated by the ReDrum is the Clap, and there's no need to route the sound.

First, adjust the sound of the Clap on the ReDrum. On the channel to the ReDrum House Kit, move the Vel knob (next to the Level knob) to the twelve o'clock position. This will bypass the velocity settings and give you a better signal to work with. Also, increase Level to 106.

Now, select the ReDrum with the House Kit patch. Choose the M-Class compressor in the Create drop-down menu and double-click the label on the M-Class Compressor to type in Comp Clap.

Next, set a loop from Bar 65 to Bar 73 and solo Channel 4, the Comp Clap track.

The Input Gain control allows you to alter the loudness of the signal coming into the compressor.

The Threshold controls when the compressor begins working. Anything below the threshold is ignored and this signal passes through, unaffected.

The Ratio controls how much compression is being added. A 2:1 ratio means that for every two dB the signal goes over the threshold, the compressor outputs one dB.

The Attack controls how quickly the compressor reacts. With the attack all the way to the left, the compressor is set to its fastest setting and the signal is compressed immediately. Your shifting the compressor's attack to the right slows down the attack, allowing for more of the original transient to come through.

The Release controls how quickly the compressor returns back to its nominal level. With a faster release, you can obtain a nice rhythmic feel, but a slower release will smooth out the sound. Both are useful, depending on the type of signal being compressed.

The Output Gain enables you to make up any lost volume due to height compression ratios.

I always approach the setting up of the compressor in the same way. It doesn't matter if it's a hardware or software compressor, as they are all designed to work in the same way.

Start by increasing Ratio to its highest setting. This may seem a bit extreme, but it really allows you to hear the compressor. Next, adjust the Attack and Release controls to their fastest settings. Now, increase the Input Gain no more than 6 dB and adjust the Threshold (–24.1 dB) so you're seeing a reading of between 8 and 12 on the Gain Reduction meter.

Start bringing up the Attack to 68 ms. Notice how the initial transient of the hit comes through and the sound now has more presence. Next, increase the Release all the way up and slowly begin decreasing it. What you're looking, or listening, for is the rhythm of the compressor. If it is too slow, it squashes the sound. Because the sound is a short burst, you want a fast release of 101 ms. Now that you've found the rhythm of the compressor, bring down the ratio to 6.20:1. You should be getting a reading of about –3 dB on the Gain Reduction meter. Finally, bring up the Output Gain 3 dB to compensate for the gain reduction.

Unsolo the track and set the level of the Comp Clap track on the mixer down to 56.

Reverbs, Delays, and Auxiliary Tracks

Next, set up your mixer to work with reverbs and delays. You'll accomplish this by setting up send and returns via the Aux channels.

Start by selecting the mixer and selecting the RV7000 from the Create menu.

Click the Browse Patch button and select EFX Kick Bomb from the list. Double-click the label on the RV7000 and type in Kick Bomb.

On Channel 6 of the mixer, raise the Aux 1 knob to 29. You should now be hearing a reverb effect on the JapanPluck patch.

Hit Tab on your keyboard and take a look at the routing.

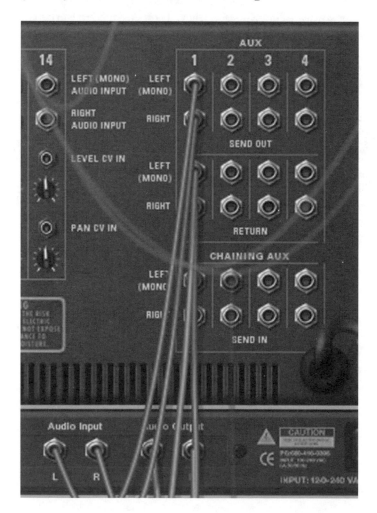

In the Aux section on the mixer, you can see cables coming from the Send Out section being routed to the Audio Input on the RV7000.

The JapanPluck signal is routed via Aux 1 Send Out, processed by the RV7000.

The processed signal of the RV7000 is routed from the Audio Out section and cabled to the Return section of the mixer.

Press the Tab key to view the front of the rack.

The return level is controlled by Knob 1 of the Return section.

Let's create two additional effects to use on your mixer. With the mixer selected, use the Create menu to create a DDL-1 and another RV7000.

On the DDL-1, click the Up button next to the numerical display until it reads 6. This sets a delay time of sixth notes. Double-click on the DDL-1 label and type in Delay 1/6.

On the RV7000, click the Patch Browser button and select the patch EKO SpaceEcho 2. Double-click on the label and type in Echo 1/16.

Using Sends from the ReDrum

Another useful feature of the ReDrum is the ability to chain its corresponding aux sends to the mixer. The routing was already done for you when you created the first ReDrum. Now, if you Tab around to reveal the back, you see the Send Out of ReDrum 1 is cabled to the Chaining Aux input of the mixer. This allows you to send any of the drum sounds of the ReDrum to Aux 1 and 2 on the mixer.

Select a loop from Bar 9 to Bar 17 and press Play.

Bring the level up on Channel 3 to 73 of the ReDrum. This is the sound of the "rev crash" that you're using as a transitional accent. Next, bring the S1 (Send 1) knob to 79 on the Channel 3 of the ReDrum.

Now you hear the Rev Crash sound, and with more clarity and greater depth.

Next, on the ReDrum, increase the level of the High Hat, Channel 9, to 70. Also, bring up S1 and S2 of Channel 9 to 22. This will bring out the High Hat a little, as well as add a little depth. Finally, bring up the S1 of Channel 2 to 20.

Now, set a loop for the breakdown section, which is located from Bar 48.4.1.0 to Bar 65.

Sweetening with Aux Sends

Make the following settings on the mixer:

At this point, you now have a pretty balanced and decent-sounding mix. In the next chapter, you will take a closer look at how you can use automation to layer in some additional dynamic mixing and effects to really bring this track to life.

Chapter 11
AUTOMATION

What Is Automation?

Automation is one feature that is often overlooked, especially by the beginning producer. This feature allows for a greater depth of control for your mixes and arrangement. Before automation, you would literally have to grab several people and assign each person a task while the song was playing back. With the advent of MIDI and computer-based sequencing programs such as Reason, you now have the power to automate every conceivable parameter available in an arrangement or mix. Moreover, you can edit the automation data so that their timing is absolutely perfect.

There are several ways to automate the mix parameters. The simplest is to draw in the automation, using the Pencil tool. However, a much more expressive and fun way is to record automation in real time as you play back your song.

Automation in Reason is really quite easy. Although it is possible to record parameter automation into a preexisting clip, I like to keep things simple and use a separate note lane onto which to record the parameter automation.

Let's start by automating the Modulation wheel on the Malstrom Gangsta Lead track.

If you have a MIDI controller with a Modulation wheel, this has already mapped, so you can just press Record and grab the physical control to make a pass. But if your controller doesn't have a Mod wheel, then you can grab the virtual one found in the Malstrom interface.

Getting Started with Automation

The Modulation wheel is the second wheel to the right (the first being the Pitch Bend, located on the left).

Recording Automation

Let's begin by creating a new note lane. With the track selected, click New Note Lane from the Edit menu. A new lane will appear above the lane where you recorded the note data. Record-arm the lane and move your song position line (SPL) to where you'd like to start to record. For this particular recording, I'm going to place the SPL to just before the note clip. Press Record on the Transport window and record the movements of the Modulation wheel.

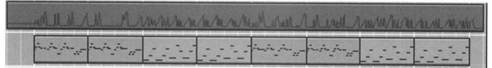

Here are your newly recorded Modulation wheel automation data. Just like a note clip, if you double-click on this, it will open in the Edit, view where you can both view and edit the data.

Editing Automation

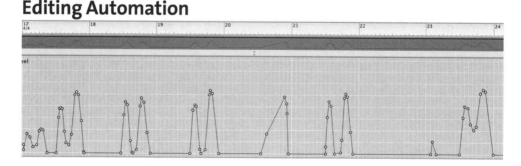

The automation data can easily be edited by selecting the nodes (the tiny circles). You can select a node and move it up, down, or side to side. It won't allow you to move beyond another node, but you can select a node and delete it, using the Delete key on your keyboard. You can also rubber-band select around multiple nodes and delete an entire section of data. By your holding down the Command key on your computer keyboard, the Selector tool will toggle to the Pencil tool. This makes fast work of editing, as you can very quickly switch back and forth between drawing and selecting. Because the automation data is contained within a note clip, you can use the Snap function to match your automation to the grid, which allows for extremely tight performance and editing.

After you've edited your data into a perfect take, you can now move back to the

Arrangement window and cut and paste the automation into different areas of your song.

Right-Clicking to Create Automation Lane

Another quick way of automating parameters is to create an automation lane by right-clicking on a parameter and selecting Edit Automation. In this example, I right-clicked over the Aux Send 3 of Channel 4 of the mixer.

The result is the creation of a new lane in the sequencer window. You can now record the Aux Send movements in real time or draw in data using the Pencil tool.

This time I chose to draw in a four-bar blank clip, using the Pencil tool, after pressing the Edit button and penciling in automation over the last "clap" of the four-bar clip.

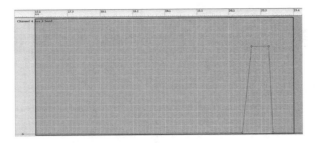

I then copied the automation to cover the main A and B parts of the song, from Bar 17 to Bar 49 and Bar 65 to Bar 97.

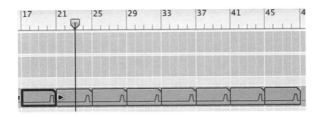

Note that automated parameters will be displayed with a green border.

Let's add some additional ear candy by automating S2 of Channel 2 on the DnB Kit. Make sure the Rec Ready button on the DnB Kit is not selected. Press Record on the Transport window, bring S2 up to 75, and let it play till the end of the song. You'll now have a subtle delay on the Snare hit that adds a counterrhythm to the break down and the last half of your track.

Deleting Automation

If you are using separate note lanes to add automation, an easy way to delete data is to select the clip and hit Delete on your computer keyboard. Another quick way of deleting all automation from a particular lane is by right-clicking on the parameter (outlined in green) and selecting Clear Automation.

Chapter 12

FINALIZING AND EXPORTING

What Is Mastering?

Mastering is the final step in audio production before your project is sent for mass reproduction. The process entails critical listening within an acoustically designed room and employs the use of high-end audio equipment to fix any anomalies that may be present in the mix. A mastering engineer will also balance out the loudness of each track so that the overall collection of songs or album will flow properly. Mastering engineers have also been known to help with the order of tracks on an album. They lend an objective, experienced take on your music. The end result is polished and professional. Luckily, Reason ships with the M-Class Mastering Suite, a collection of excellent-sounding plugins that will give your track that professional polish.

Using the M-Class Mastering Suite Combi

The last process you will engage for your song before mixing down is to use the default mastering suite, which consists of a Combinator with an M-Class EQ, Stereo Imager, Compressor, and Maximizer. This final element of your track will ultimately give it a finished polish. Bear in mind, if you plan to send your track to a mastering engineer—something I highly recommend—you'll want to go easy on these effects, as the mastering engineer will be similarly adding his or her own magic. When sending tracks out to a mastering engineer, make sure you are delivering a premaster version of the data.

A premaster is a finished track, but contains little compression or EQ on the stereo bus and has at least 5 dB of headroom, which will allow the engineer to make the track sound its best.

Let's assume for now that you are going to be mastering the track yourself.

Begin by setting up a loop containing the entire song.

There are several different mastering presets. Many are useful for different genres of music, so feel free to explore some of them. For the purposes of this tutorial, you'll be using the default mastering suite.

Setting up the M-Class Mastering Suite

You're going to use the controls at the top of the Combinator interface with some additional tweaking on specific devices within the Combi.

Engaging the Big Meter

Start by selecting the Big Meter, located on the Hardware Interface. Next, make sure you select the Audio Output 1–2 to engage the Big Meter. Once you have routed the signal through the meter, deselect the Audio I/O button to remove some of the clutter within the interface.

Activating the Components and Setting Levels

Next, activate the Stereo Imager and the Compressor on the Combi interface.

    The Stereo Imager will allow you the focus the low-frequency content while adding some width to the upper mid- and high-frequency content.

    The compressor will help smooth out the mix by subtly evening out the overall loudness of your mix. Keep in mind "less is more"; the last thing you want to do is overcompress the track, resulting in a flat, lifeless mix.

Increase the loudness curve to 62. This will add an additional boost of low and high frequencies to the overall mix.

Now adjust the compression to 67. This will change the threshold to about –19 dB and the ratio to 2.3:1.

Deselect the Lo Cut filter on the EQ and set Master Gain to 56.

Engage the Punch button. If you notice any digital clipping on the Big Meter, engage the 4 ms Look Ahead button on the Maximizer. Let's also change the attack to Fast on the Maximizer. You are now ready to export your song and begin the mixing-down process.

Exporting your Song

Now you'll learn how to export your song so you can share it with the world.

End of Song Marker

The first thing you need to do is set the End of Song marker. Make sure to listen to your track once with the loop function off. You want to make sure that the reverb tail on the JapanPluck track decays out to silence. If not, the reverb will be cut short and the sound will end too abruptly. Note how I have set the E marker to just past Bar 113.

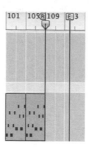

Export Song

Next, select Export Song as Audio File from the File menu.

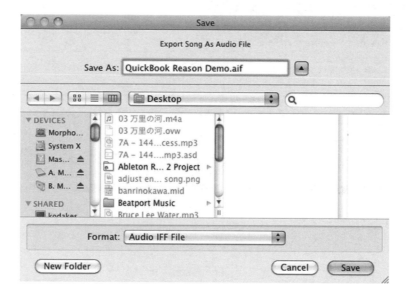

Name the Song

A dialog box will open for you to name the song. I chose the title Quickbook Reason Demo. You can also choose what format with which to export the data. The choices available are .aiff or .wav files. Either one is fine, as they are essentially the same in quality. The default file for Mac is AIFF, whereas WAV is used for Windows-based PCs.

Once you've selected the correct format, click the Save button.

Export Settings

The next window you will see is Audio Export Settings. You can select your sample rate, bit depth, and whether or not you want to use Dither.

Sample Rate

I'd like to burn this song on to a CD, so I need to confirm that Sample Rate is set correctly. The settings range from 11,025 Hz to 192,000 Hz. The standard sample rate for an audio CDs is 44,100 Hz, which is also happens to be the default setting.

Bit Depth

The Bit Depth setting gives you the option of either 24- or 16-bit settings. The 24-bit setting provides higher quality and would be ideal if you're sending this to a mastering engineer or want to import the song into another program. Sixteen bits, however, is the standard for audio CDs—and is also the default setting.

Dither

Dithering is a process you would use to get from a 24-bit file to a 16-bit file without any loss in quality. Imagine for a moment, that your session is 24 bits. If you choose to export the audio at 16 bits without using Dither, the program will chop off the top 8 bits, thereby affecting the quality of the export.

This is when Dithering can come to the rescue. The process of Dithering involves adding super-high-frequency noise into your file. The high frequency is well above human hearing, so you can't actually hear it. Now, when the program needs to remove 8 bits, it removes the high-frequency noise and the result is a 16-bit file that sounds like your 24-bit file.

Since I'm burning this song to a CD, I'm going to keep Dither on and hit Export.

Export

Next, you'll see the Export Audio progress gauge.

Your song appears as a file on the desktop.

APPENDIX: THE DVD-ROM

On the enclosed DVD-ROM, I have included thirteen videos to help you get acquainted with Reason. In addition, I've also included three Reason song files to help with Chapter 9, "Creating an Arrangement"; Chapter 10, "The Art and Science of Mixing"; and Chapter 12, "Finalizing and Exporting."

Video Tutorials

The following tutorials are designed to accompany The Power in Reason to help clarify and cement certain topics throughout the book.

1. Reason Overview

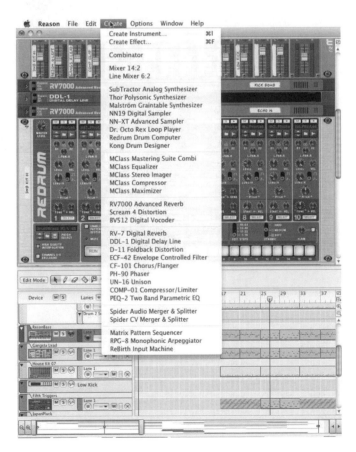

This video provides a quick overview of the software, including menu structures, the rack, sequencer window, and transport.

2. Instrument Overview (Synthesizers)

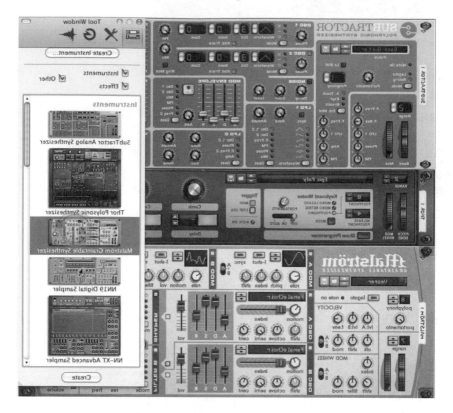

The instrument overview video has been broken up into three parts. Each part covers a basic overview of the instruments and what type of sounds you can expect from each.

This first part covers Reason's synthesizers, the Subtractor, Thor, and Malstrom.

3. Instrument Overview (Samplers)

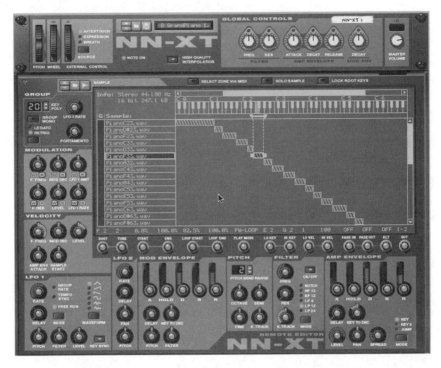

Part two of the instrument overview covers Reason's samplers, the NN19, and the NN-XT.

4. Instrument Overview (Drums)

The final part of the instrument overview covers the Drum modules, including the Dr. OctoRex, ReDrum, and Kong Drum Synthesizer.

5. Reason FX

This video provides a basic overview of Reason's effects.

6. Basic Recording

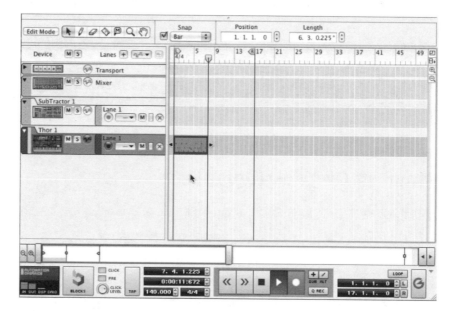

This video covers the basics of recording and editing MIDI.

7. Sequencing Drums

This video covers programming drums with the ReDrum drum machine.

8. Matrix Pattern Sequencing

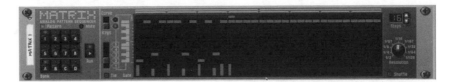

This video covers the setup and use of the Matrix Pattern Sequencer.

9. RPG-8 Arpeggiator

This video covers the setup and use of the RPG-8 Arpeggiator.

10. Arrangement Tips

This video provides an overview to the chapter on arranging.

11. Mixing Tips

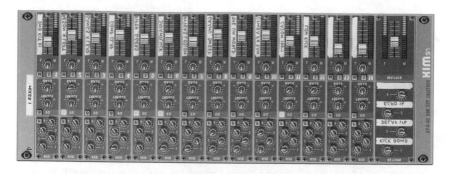

This video provides an overview to the chapter on mixing. topics, including the use of EQ and compression.

12. Automation

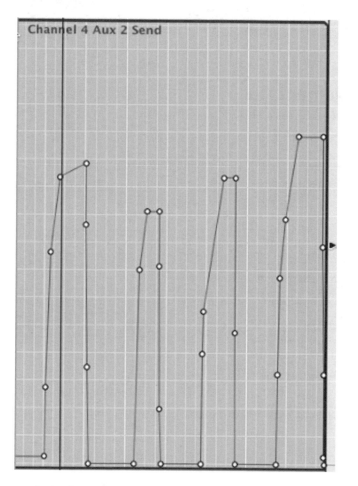

This video covers the basics on how to set up the sequencer to record automation.

13. Mastering FX and Mixdown

The final video covers Reason's mastering effects and how to mix down your song.

Reason Song Files

The following three song files are to be used in conjunction with their respective chapters.

Chapter 9—Creating an Arrangement.rns

This song file contains two MIDI clips, which can be substituted for the process of recording the A and B parts within Chapter 9.

Chapter 10—Mixing.rns

This song file contains the completed arrangement without mixing or automation. It may also be used to check your work for Chapter 9.

Final Mix.rns

This song file is the final version of the song, complete with mixing, automation, and mastering effects applied.

Reason Song 1.aff

This is an AIFF file bounced down from the Final Mix.rns song file.

Index